Olivia Precious Cooper

Hannah
PRAYED

And Changed Destiny

Hannah PRAYED

And Changed Destiny

Olivia Precious Cooper

IAP Publishing

Hannah PRAYED: And Changed Destiny
Copyright © 2017 Olivia Precious Cooper
Published by IAP Publishing
A division of I Am Precious International Harvest Ministries
Email: publishing@preciousinternational.org
Website: https://www.preciousinternational.org
Phone: +1(615) 669-6460

All rights reserved. This book is protected under the copyright laws of the United States of America. This book or part thereof may not be reproduced in any form, stored in a retrieval system, or transmitted in any form by any means electronic, mechanical, photocopying, recording, or otherwise without prior written permission of the publisher.

Unless otherwise identified, Scripture is taking from THE HOLY BIBLE, King James Version.
"Scripture quotations taken from the Amplified® Bible (AMP), Copyright © 2015 by The Lockman Foundation. Used by permission. www.Lockman.org"

ISBN-10: 0-9830157-9-1
ISBN-13: 978-0-9830157-9-6
Designs by IAP Publishing

Printed in the United States of America

Quantity Sales: Special discounts are available on quantity purchased by ministries, associations, and others. For details, contact the publisher at the above address.

DEDICATION

I dedicate this book to the Watchers and Holy Ones; to the Apostles and Prophets of Old; to the Laborers sent out by FATHER into the Harvest. to the Remnant yet to Manifest; to my Spiritual Covering and Kingdom Helpers; to the Sons and Daughters God entrusts to my service.

Table of Contents

Introduction 1

The Situation 13

The Enemy 33

The Family 53

The Priest 71

The Flesh 85

   The Root of Bitterness 89

The Meeting 105

The Answers 123

ACKNOWLEDGMENT

Hannah Prayed is a Masterpiece. Not because I wrote it, but because He gave it to me. Thus, if there is someone to acknowledge, it is Holy Spirit.

Only He could have opened my eyes to see into Hannah's life. Only He could have given the ability to pen such revelations.

Holy Spirit, I love and honor You. Thank You for finding me worthy to serve Your people. Thank You for all You have done and will do through

Hannah **PRAYED**: *And Changed Destiny.*

Introduction

1

You are about to embark upon a spiritual journey to answered prayers regardless of whether you are a man or woman. Hannah Prayed is not for women only. This book will take you from the answers you think you need, to the destiny God desires for you. Let me begin by warning you that this is not a message about formulas to teach how to get material things, but a true story that portrays processes we must go through in order to change destinies.

I lay a foundation by pointing to what Jesus said in John 4:24, "God is a Spirit: and they that worship Him must worship Him in spirit and in truth." Likewise, our prayers must also be *in spirit and truth*. We are to engage in prayer with the objective of fulfilling God's Will, for it is our true worship unto Him and in Him.

This is life in the Spirit of God, and every believer's life is in this realm of spirituality. It is from the spiritual that we will arrive at the physical so desired. It is from the life within that we birth the life worth living without. Our obedience to God is our worship in spirit and truth. God's desire is our destiny, and through the processing of prayer, we will arrive there.

You, my dear reader, may have never seen prayer as a process one must go through in order to change destinies. Notwithstanding, this is how it has always been and will always be with prayer, as long as we are reaching into God's Kingdom to establish it on earth. The Lord began to open my eyes and speak to me about this more powerfully as I prepared to minister for a women's conference some years ago.

The theme of the conference was about prayer, in particular, Hannah's prayer. At first, I thought my message would be about how Hannah got what she wanted through prayer, a child. Little did I know then that God's message was about His plan concerning Israel being fulfilled through Hannah by leading her to pray. Big difference! That is what He wants you to learn through this book.

As God uses me in the office of a prophet, I've come to discover that people like to receive prophecies of material and emotional things like money, houses, marriages, etc. However, it is expedient to receive the Mind of God concerning your spiritual life and destiny. If you hear about God giving you material things, thank Him for them. But make conscious efforts to redirect your mind to remain focused on Him. Let your prayers be about Him; how to fulfil His desire and plans, not yours. Understand that you are a spiritual being with a spiritual life of worship to God.

You may have a career that you are pursuing, but what is the spiritual path that you must be on? Because, that is where God is most concerned. What territories are you taking for the Kingdom? Or are you just concerned about getting the next million dollar home? Listen, God wants us to have all good and earthly things, but that is not His prime interest towards us. So, why make it yours!

The house, car, and everything else that is materially and emotionally fulfilling, cannot do warfare on your behalf when it comes to the enemy you face. For example, when God says that *He prepares a table before us in the presence of your enemies,* oftentimes, people think that it's concerning the blissfulness and the luxuries of the human life. Unfortunately for them, they miss the point because that is not what God is saying. That interpretation is the voice of a carnal or spiritually immature mind that cannot discern spiritual things.

If spiritual things are not discerned spiritually, the individual will experience disappointments in terms of expectations. Why would God prepare a table of physical things in the presence of one's enemies when He knows that such things are not Kingdom inheritance? Not only that, our fights are not against flesh and blood, but against demonic and satanic spirits operating from the kingdom of darkness. Thus, we use spiritual weapons for spiritual battles.

Furthermore, a table prepared before us is a place where we can sit and sup with the Lord, eating Revelations of His Word as He feeds us. Christ says in Revelation 3:20, *"Behold, I stand at the door, and knock: if any man hear my voice, and open the door, I will come in to him, and will sup with him, and he with me."* I encourage you to take a moment and read His entire message to the Church at Laodicea, because you will see that people in that church state were deceived into thinking that having material things meant being spiritually rich. Jesus rebuked them and told them to repent of such ways of thinking and living.

Thus, a table prepared before us is His Word being delivered to us in the presence of the enemies so that He can use that Word working in us to destroy the enemy facing us and even within us. This to us also symbolizes our intimate relationship with the Lord. In addition, it is a sign to the enemies of darkness that God is on our side, in us, and with us against them. And by the way, they are not invited to sup at this table.

With the understanding of spiritually discerning spiritual things, we will do so concerning the life of the exemplary character of this book. Hannah, a woman of prayer! Isn't that the conclusion of this Biblical character when she is spoken of? We know her to be the mother who birth Israel's great prophet, Samuel. If you have come across some history of who she was, I have no doubt that she is portrayed as a woman who gained victory through prayers over her taunting mate, Peninnah.

When you think about Hannah, you may think of a mighty woman of prayer. Hannah prayed and something happened. She was fired up. She prayed, and many want to be like Hannah to some degree, since she prayed and she received the answer. Logically, that is what comes to mind? But is that what really happened and is it all that occurred?

You may not comprehend this now, but I tell you the truth when I say, that is not all there is to Hannah's story if you're discerning spiritually. It takes the Spirit of Revelation and Understanding to grasp the deeper things of God. As you read along, you will experience Holy Spirit giving you the necessities to understand what I'm sharing.

Note that through revelation comes purging. God is going to open you up, and in doing so, you will be able to recognize filthy characteristics of the flesh from Hannah's life and probably yours. I'm talking about issues like the root of bitterness, selfishness, anger, and other deeply entrenched matters of the heart and defilements of spirit. The awesome thing is that those fleshy things seen or experienced as a result of receiving this message are not what will remain. God's Holy Spirit will cause a great deliverance to occur for you. This is His promise!

Perhaps, you might say, I thought this book is about prayer? Yes, it is. But again, prayer is more than simply receiving answers. If your desire is to please God and do His Will, He will have to process you even through your prayers. God will not give you a divine destiny to birth if you are of the wrong root

And Changed Destiny | 6

or linked to the wrong source. Even when we have received His Mind concerning our destinies in Him, we still will have to undergo His processes of learning and testings.

The story of Hannah in the First Book of Samuel is an excellent example of how we cannot get what we want until there is a work of transformation on the inside of us. Something must change in us first. The work of transformation that results in destiny changes is a work that requires the fiery manifestations of God. Our God is like a *Refiner's Fire* and is a *Consuming Fire.* So if you are a child of God, you are going to experience these two types of Fire either at the same time or at different times. In other words, He is either going to be refining you or He is going to be consuming something inside of you.

This is hard truth that the believer must comprehend. So the next time you hear of a person on "fire" for God, or praying some fiery prayers, remember that he or she is actually dancing in the flames of God Himself; either in one dimension of consumption or another dimension of refinement, but, there's no escaping. This may sound fearful, but let it not be so in your ears. Hopefully, you will be the next one we hear about who is on "fire" for God. Hallelujah!

Some hearing of God burning things in folks might say, "Ain't nothing wrong with me that requires fire" or "No thanks, I'm good". Are you thinking the same? Well, if you do, I beg to differ and I cut that thought down in the spirit. If there was nothing wrong with you, you would be walking with Jesus where He is right now, and not reading this book. So as God has dealt with me and *is* dealing with me, I believe He is going to deal with you too.

One of the things we need to understand as the Body of Christ is that God is in the business of cutting and burning us up. Please note, that I speak symbolically and spiritually. God is in the business of getting us to be like Him, and He can only do that when we go through pains and hurts within the soulish realms. It's called *dying to self*. Therefore, God through His Word and Spirit is going to dig out what is of darkness so that He can pour in what is purely of Him. Actually, He pours in His Light first, and the darkness comes out as a result.

The Lord informs us that those whom He loves, He will chastise. Chastisement is the norm for believers living in the Spirit. It is also a way to bring about deliverance to and for the child of God. This is part of our Father's Love towards us. God is Love and this is simply a display of Who He is and how He behaves. Everything He does is out of the motivation of love. His chastising of us is to build us up and not punish us or hurt us, as some regrettably believe. In understanding further the need for chastisement, the Bible shines light on the reasons for chastisement, and even gives examples of how God has molded others by chastising them. The Amplified Bible version of Hebrews 12:7-11 states it very well:-

> *You must submit to [correction for the purpose of] discipline; God is dealing with you as with sons; for [a]what son is there whom his father does not discipline? Now if you are exempt from correction and without discipline, in which all [of God's children] share, then you are illegitimate children and not sons [at all]. Moreover, we have had earthly fathers who disciplined us, and we submitted and respected them [for training us]; shall we not much more willingly submit to the Father of [b]spirits, and live [by learning from His discipline]? For our earthly fathers disciplined us for only a short time as seemed best to them; but He disciplines us for our good, so that we may share His holiness. For the time being no discipline brings joy, but seems sad and painful; yet to those who have been trained by it, afterwards it yields the peaceful fruit of righteousness [right standing with God and a lifestyle and attitude that seeks conformity to God's will and purpose].*

Hannah was not a born-again believer in Christ as we are today, but in her day and time, she was a daughter of Israel, God's chosen people. They were without excuse when it came to the Law and being a part of God's Plan. Therefore, you will see who Hannah was and discover who Hannah became; for she also had to go through her own personal transformation and chastening of the Lord.

Through her life written in the Bible, you will see yourself. Before her prayer in Chapter one of 1st Samuel, Hannah represents a face of the believer who desires something from God. The person who wants His Hand, that is what He can give; and is naïve of His Plan, meaning what He wants to accomplish. One good thing she had going for her was that her heart did not lie, even as she prayed. God, being a Merciful and Sovercign God, eventually, allowed Hannah to experience Him, which was more than just receiving an answer to prayers.

So, what did take place before Hannah prayed and during her prayers? What was the state of her heart? When she was barren, did she love Peninnah, her mate? Was she satisfied with her husband? Did she think that the enemy had attacked her womb or maybe it was Peninnah's fault that she couldn't conceive? What was in Hannah's heart before God gave her Samuel, the answer to her prayers?

As you know, Hannah prayed and received her son. But Hannah had to first die to self. This is the process that comes as a result of prayers. Unfortunately, not many believers want to die to self. Yet, they expect God to do everything they supposedly ask for in prayers.

They think that is what prayer entails. Religion has done damage to deceive people into thinking that whatsoever they ask for in prayers, they will receive. They ask, seek, knock, fast, beg, groan, throw tantrums, sow, call all the prayer partners they can reach, attend conferences, and do whatever could be a way to move God's Hand, but nothing happens as they expect. What remains after all that is God's willingness to process them.

All self-efforts and dead works can stop once believers learn the ways of God. If they discern the Scriptures spiritually, they will understand that all of God's blessings, promises, and gifts are conditional. Each one of them comes packaged with the processing guidelines. In addition, they must fit within His overall Purpose and Divine Timing.

This message titled, **Hannah Prayed: and Changed Destiny** is a gem. It is Heaven giving you spiritual nuggets to God's Heart and strategies to get His results. From His Heart, you will get His Hand, and from His Hand you will get your life. It is never the other way around.

Like Hannah, you may have desired a son and nothing more. But if you allow God, you, like Hannah, will get more than a son. Your destiny will change and that of others; and if possible, an entire nation. Our Father is no respecter of persons, He will use any vessel willing to go through His processing.

Are you ready to birth out God's Plan? If so, let's journey on. Don't doubt yourself, and if you do, don't doubt God.

The Situation

2

The Bible introduced Hannah to us in 1 Samuel Chapter One as the wife of Elkanah, a certain man. Interestingly, Hannah happens to be perhaps his first wife since she is named first in the story before Peninnah, Elkanah's other wife. We are informed that Peninnah had children while Hannah was childless. One would think that your husband's children would be your children as well, but I guess there's nothing like your own no matter what the situation may be.

We are not told of how long Hannah had been married. But if we assume that she's the first wife, then she and Elkanah must have been married for quite some time since her mate, Peninnah, had both sons and daughters. In addition, the Bible mentions that they all went to worship and made sacrifices yearly, which further concludes that they had been married for several years.

This is very important because it highlights the length of time Hannah had been in the situation she found herself. It is apparent that it was quite a length of time, and too long to be in such misery. It is so much easier for a person to endure something when the lifespan of the situation is short. But if it's a situation that a person has to go through year after year, it can be very frustrating and even overbearing.

Childlessness, as in Hannah's case, is not a condition any person would appreciate being in for any length of time, be it short or long. Especially, being barren during the days she lived. It was almost like a taboo or a curse. That is because having children is recorded as blessings from the Lord. To many, Hannah's womb being shut would indicate that she had sinned or affected God in some way. This brought about a state of tremendous shame and reproach.

Unfortunately, being barren is not the kind of situation that can be kept a secret for long. There are things people go through and no one else will ever know about them. But a situation that has external proof such as a child or children, secrecy is difficult to achieve and almost impossible. Society will get to know, and like Hannah's predicament, I'm sure all of the neighbors knew she had such a problem. So how did she live day after day and year after year with the open shame and embarrassment? How does one in similar conditions console him or herself that all is well when deep down inside it is not?

Hannah's story of barrenness does represent the majority of people who live life in situations that are regrettably public information. Do you recall the last time you went through a situation that couldn't be hidden? Or are you in one right now? Unfortunately, going through such times would appear as though the situation is a city on a hill that cannot be hid. It will show regardless of whether we want it to or not, and nothing will pacify us until we get the answers we desire concerning the unhappy situation.

It's like one of those things that you pray about over, and over, and over again but to no avail. It's just there. This reminds me of what apostle Paul talks about in 2 Corinthians 12:7-8 when he said, *"And lest I should be exalted above measure through the abundance of the revelations, there was given to me a thorn in the flesh, the messenger of Satan to buffet me, lest I should be exalted above measure. For this thing I besought the Lord thrice, that it might depart from me."* But it did not go away. Paul assumed that God would have answered him after seeking three different times to remove something as bad as the messenger of Satan. Oh, but no, God simply said that His grace was very sufficient for him.

What does grace have to do with a demon beating Paul? How did that help his situation? Did he not pray enough or did he pray amiss? Definitely, not Paul the apostle. He understood prayer and he knew how to pray.

Conclusively, Paul prayed and received an answer according to God's divine plan. Paul understood what grace was and how to apply it to his situation. Thus, he resolved that what he needed was more of the processing the situation produced, than simply the rebuking of the evil spirit. He learned that in order to experience the strength of the Lord over his situation, he had to acknowledge, accept, and glory in his weakness. A weakness that was inevitably his strength; his dependency on God. In other words, Paul had to see God's heart at work in his life, and not just the relief he so desired from his temporary situation.

When it comes to Hannah, she was in a situation which consumed her. Her lack or what I could say, her weakness, became a situation that brought her sorrow, dissatisfaction, envy, and bitterness. I'm sure she had prayed, and prayed, and prayed with no answer forthcoming about her expectations of a child. What she did not see was God at work behind the scene to change destinies.

Hannah was so immersed in her childless situation that she no longer was experiencing joy from other things in her life. Her need and the lack thereof blinded her. Not even her husband's affections were satisfying, simply because she did not have exactly what she wanted. She wanted a child and anything other than a child was not good enough.

Hannah's husband, Elkanah, loved her dearly and always gave her a worthy portion. In other words, she received more from him then Peninnah. I will not go into the possible reasons that prompted his love for Hannah now. We will discuss it in a later Chapter. But what I want you to realize concerning the situation, is that Hannah was loved by him regardless of her barrenness.

Why was giving birth to a child so pressing in Hannah's life? Could it have been because of the promising destiny of her child that was to be born? At times we are not conscious as to why we so desperately want certain things but we do. To us, our desperation is to fulfill and satisfy a need, but little do we realized that there is something more which could be prompting us further and further into desperation.

Like Hannah, we all fall into desperate situations that call for desperate measures. As believers, we find ourselves pressing in prayer, pushing until something happens. And it can be consuming, stealing each moment of our day and focus. But regardless of how desperate a person may become, nothing should consume them except a desire for God.

Another character in the Bible who was desperate for a child was Rachel. She was Jacob's second wife, which should have been his first, but there was foul play from her father during the wedding and Jacob ended up marrying Leah instead of Rachel. They did marry, and their marriage was good and birthed out of love when it finally took place seven years later.

Similarly to Hannah, Rachel's mate and sister, Leah, had had more than five children while she had none. To make matters worse for Rachel, Leah had more children by her handmaids. Rachel also used the same strategy of giving her handmaid to Jacob to give her children. But regardless, Rachel needed her own. In conclusion to the situation at that time, Leah was very fruitful leaving Rachel very barren both physically and psychologically.

Jacob, like Elkanah, loved his barren wife, Rachel, and he showed it. His love for her was so visible that Leah had children just to get a little more of Jacob's attention. Rachel who had almost all of Jacob's attention, was not settling to living without giving Jacob a child. Fortunately for her, she had two boys. Her prayers were answered but she died while giving birth to her second son.

Both Rachel's and Hannah's childbearing and situations had key roles in the plan and future of Israel. Their desires were bigger than themselves. To them, they needed what was normal for any married woman. They were both in circumstances that required fulfillment of their responsibilities as wives and women. They were not seeking anything out of the norm. But would it have been easier for them if they had known that their barrenness was beyond them? What would have happened to them emotionally if they were conscious that their weakness was a part of God's divine timetable? Would they have lived their lives differently? The answers to these questions are not clear, but I do say that the condition of their hearts would have been better.

Situations in life have a way of changing people, and oftentimes, for the worse. This is not God's way and neither is it His desire. His plan in every situation is always to bring us to a glorious end. But to make the situation easier to endure, we will have to know some of God's ways and at least have an idea of His plan for us. This is why He says in Jeremiah 29:11, *"For I know the thoughts that I think toward you, saith the LORD, thoughts of peace, and not of evil, to give you an expected end."* David also in Psalm 40:5 echoes, *"Many, O LORD my God, are thy wonderful works which thou hast done, and thy thoughts which are to us-ward: they cannot be reckoned up in order unto thee: if I would declare and speak of them, they are more than can be numbered."*

Children of God will always go through trials, temptations, testings, sufferings, and even tribulations. The end result is to come out as overcomers having overcome whatever needed overcoming. We do not pray, "God get us out" but rather, *"Lord, not my will but Your will be done"* (Luke 22:42). This is what Jesus prayed when He was in the worst situation any human has ever experienced. Although He prayed three times in the Garden of Gethsemane that God would take the situation of going to the cross away from Him, Father did not give Him that answer because it would have brought a temporary relief for His flesh and destruction to His Purpose. Instead, God kept Him through the processing of prayer. And it resulted in destinies being changed as predestinated by God.

When God is at work, every person in every situation must align to His ultimate agenda. Hannah and her situation were no different. Even though Hannah did not know the bigger picture behind her barrenness, God did not change His Mind concerning His ultimate purpose no matter how much Hannah was dissatisfied. She was very important in God's eyes, and so exceptionally relevant was her life to His plan that He allowed her to go through the situation.

To God, it was more than just giving Hannah a child as an answer to prayers. It was about giving Israel a mouthpiece for Himself who would honor Him and do according to the Lord's Will. On this note, it is impossible to end this Chapter on *the situation* Hannah found herself in without making mention of *the situation* Israel was in as a nation. Israel needed Hannah's situation as equally as Hannah needed Israel's situation.

We are all connected in some way or another as it pertains to the Divine Plan of God. Every piece of our lives as children of God is a 'puzzle-key' or part of a puzzle that is 'key' to the big picture. Whether you know it or not, you play a major role in and for the Kingdom of God. By the unfolding of things through prayer, you will understand how everything does work together for your good in Christ Jesus. With confidence, you should be able to say like Apostle Paul did in Romans 8:28, *"And we know that all things work together for good to them that love God, to them who are the called according to His purpose."*

This is what we see from the life of Hannah. It was not by coincidence that Hannah's family went to the Temple for the yearly worship and sacrifices during the days of Eli, the priest. This was clearly destiny changing hands. The new was coming in while the old was on its way out. Because of the changes which were about to occur, Hannah found her situation prolonged. I'm certain that at some point in her life, she thought that God was not hearing her prayers. Oh, but He was.

He heard her every cry for a child, just as He heard the cry of Israel for righteousness. Eli had two sons who were an absolute disgrace to God, their father, and the entire priesthood of Israel. God had warned Eli about the waywardness and sins of his sons, and instructed him to get his house in order. The behaviors of the boys were noticeable to many, leading to abominable acts that could not be hidden. They were the talk of all Israel.

They had become priests because they were sons of a priest, and the high priest for that matter. The priesthood could only be conferred upon one who was born in the tribe of Levi, and met certain standards. God had ordained this tribe for the Levitical priesthood. Consequently, not anyone could be a priest.

Unfortunately, Hophni and Phinehas, the sons of Eli were so evil that the Bible called them sons of Belial, a false god, because they did not know the one and only true God of Israel. First Samuel Chapter 2 highlights the abominable things they did which included demanding the Lord's portions of the sacrifices for themselves, committing adultery with women at the Temple, making the people abhor the offering, and refusing to repent. The boys needed to die and they received the just punishments for their sins.

By now you should be able to see that Hannah was not the only one desperately seeking. God, Himself, had to intervene in order to uphold His covenant with Israel. Had He not, Hannah's delivery of a child would never have been as meaningful as it was to her and the whole of Israel. It's needful to say that everything had to fall in line accordingly.

When counseling, I often encourage individuals to know that all things will conform to the perfect will of God. I tell them to look for God's invisible Hand working behind the scene to put everything in place that is needed for a successful outcome to the situation they find themselves in. Because, if a person looks at the situation from God's perspective, he or she will better succeed in the process being fulfilled.

God is more concerned about the relationship between He and us as we go through life, than what we can get to satisfy our earthly needs. Each situation is designed to bring about an outcome that fosters our relationship with the Lord, and helps us live out the roles we have to play in His plan. Notwithstanding, we must be mindful that the plan is inclusive of more than us.

Take for example a young student aspiring to be a doctor. This dream will not happen overnight because there are set progressions to follow and succeed in. Things like the required amount of schooling, the successful passing of all examinations, and the opportunities for practice must be satisfied. Inasmuch as this former student does become a certified doctor, he or she will have to wait for someone to get ill before the doctoring can occur. Every aspect must come together and play its part in the overall picture of him or her being a successful doctor. Now this is an earthly career example. How much more are we as believers who are called and destined to be kings, priests, and sons of God? Every component has to synchronize as one melodious creation of who we are called to be.

Yes, Hannah's situation was difficult for any woman to go through. In fact, the lack of something that is a normal part of life turns to a severely painful struggle. No one can blame Hannah for being dissatisfied with how life treated her. She was in a situation that was beyond her. Hannah was in God's Plan.

At this point, I encourage you to sit back and take a look at your life, especially, the things that you are praying about. How many times have you asked God in prayer for answers and still cannot testify of a change to the situation? If the lack of receiving the answer you desire has led you to become bitter and lose your joy in any way whatsoever, repent. Change your mind so that you can get a glimpse of the bigger picture. This is what repentance is, the changing of the mind.

Is there something more that God wants to accomplish through you, which has allowed you to become encircled by the circumstances you find yourself? What role will the answer to your prayer play that could change a destiny when you finally receive it? Think deeper. Are there other situations that are indirectly and even directly pulling on you for answers? Perhaps, you are a part of something bigger than you can now see.

There was a time in my life that I found myself in a situation I could not understand. God had revealed to me bits and pieces of what was going to take place. My mind immediately rushed into concluding the matter and visualizing how things would unfold. I began to pray and target my prayer towards the outcomes that I had made for myself.

You see, my dearly beloved brother or sister, if we are not careful, we might take ourselves out of the perfect will of God for our lives. God can be saying one thing, whereby, our minds are concluding something completely different as an outcome to what God is saying. This was my dilemma and I had a very difficult time going through it.

I made a call to someone in order to talk about what I was going through with hopes of receiving a little understanding. Instead of maturely voicing out my concerns, I heard myself complaining as a result of nothing seeming to work. My spiritual father whom I had phoned, Apostle Asibor, told me very frankly and sternly that, "My attitude can be a minus to my promotion." He further went on to remind me that God had me in that situation as a key piece of the puzzle and not the puzzle itself.

Ah! I was upset at the end of our conversation and desperately began to pray to God for more answers. Actually, I was completely confused and angry. It was a painful night of prayer and tears. After releasing heavy drops from the agony I was in, Jesus came and sat on the bed, and begin to talk to me. I was hurting and in desperate need for relief. I just couldn't understand what had been happening, and I surely could not appreciate why Apostle Asibor spoke to me the way he did on the phone. But now that I was with Jesus, I was certain to take advantage of the moment. And thus, I poured out my heart, and He answered my prayers. Looking back, I bless God for the reply He gave and not the answers I wanted to hear.

Up until today, I am still amazed at what the Lover of my Soul said to me. It wasn't some deep revelation or something I had not heard before. No. His answers were words to process me. As Jesus talked to me, I wasn't quite sure whether I was being rebuked or not. It was so comforting and peaceful. All I could feel at that moment was the experience of being in His Presence. I was so awestruck that He had come and literally made Himself known, that nothing else matter, whether a rebuke or not. But knowing Jesus, I was being rebuked. In addition, Apostle Asibor was very correct in what he had said to me and how he said it. I repented immediately.

My repentance led me to accept the process within the circumstances God orchestrated. My submission to the process rendered me understanding of all that was happening in the situation, including the conversation with my spiritual father. Every part of the situation were pieces of the puzzle to process me while I too was a piece of the puzzle for the situation I was in. The answers I received from both voices I submitted to, transformed my heart and changed destinies. But, before that could happen, I had to see the bigger picture.

I had to see what God wanted to fulfill from the situation and learn how to adjust myself, including my attitude, so that the end result was glorious. Again, I was a part of a puzzle that was bigger than me. Nevertheless, I could not fulfill the role of being a puzzle piece, until I had received the required processing needed prior to being fitted in the puzzle. God fitting me into the bigger picture, mandated perfection for that role. I had to come out as a fine piece of the puzzle and not a rough-edged, unprocessed piece.

Now, in case you're wondering what Jesus said to me, I'll keep most of it as my secret but share this important bit with you. What He said was, "Learn from Me as your Big Brother. Do it the way I did it. I humbled Myself ". Those words were heaven on earth to me. I ended that situation far differently than what I had expected it to be and far better. Though I had one day left on that trip, that last day was filled with joy unspeakable. Not because something in the day changed, but because, something in me was transformed. Praise be to God.

Hannah was a part of something spiritually grand, and she had to be processed for it by the situations that accumulated within her life. May your life and the situations you go through turn out the way God desires them. Don't let your attitude become a minus to your progress. And definitely do not wait to understand before you obey or submit. My beloved daughter, Prophetess Tanesha, always shares with our group that she doesn't wait to understand first. She accepts it regardless of whether she understands or not. In doing so, she receives understanding. I believe that this is the way of the sons of God.

You have to understand that it is our selfish nature that tries to interfere with the sweet and holy flow of the Spirit of God in our lives. If we are not careful, our flesh will dictate to the situations and misdirect them. Oh yes, the flesh will speak to you and the situation, because it is trying to be in control. So that what is intended to be something meaningful and purposeful, ends up becoming detrimental. A situation designed by God to bring about changes in destinies could face a potential threat of destruction simply because we allow the flesh and its demands to blind us. I pray this is not your portion.

Hannah did not know that her condition intercepted at a point with Israel's future. But thank God that His Will prevailed. Regardless of her not being able to change the situation when and how she wanted it changed, she still did what was best, and it was to continuously pray. It was through her prayers that she went past the situation, and this is what you and I will always have to do; *go past the situation.*

Always see situations as packages prepared to take you deeper into the processes of God, and further along your journey of destiny. Each situation carries its unique set of tools to move us, but they should not consume us. They are there as precedents to justify the outcomes of God working in our lives. If the situation in Israel's priestly line did not require the removal of Eli and his sons, the need for Hannah's son as a vital role in Israel's future would have been pointless. You will see later on in chapters to follow that there was a purpose even to the barrenness of Hannah.

Allow your life to have meaning beyond you. Allow your prayers to have influence in the spiritual realms as you set your heart on God's Ultimate Plan. The answers you seek will become vitally important in the physical realm because they will be Heaven on earth.

Hannah was successful in getting past the situation, not the way she planned but the way God worked and transformed her heart. Ahead, you will see how Hannah went past the enemy, family, self, and even the priest in order to meet with God and receive His answers for her and Israel.

The Enemy

3

Can this book be complete without investigating the enemy and what role the kingdom of darkness played? In fact, was the enemy a part of the situation that Hannah found herself in? Many might quickly jump to the conclusion that it was the enemy that inflicted barrenness upon her and render no explanation or justification as to why. Whether the problem that Hannah went through was caused by an enemy or not, there must be absolute Biblical grounds to warrant that verdict.

Before a person can go after a possibly responsible party, he or she will have to inquire of the possibilities of that person or thing being present and involved. There's a joke that claims that satan is in a corner somewhere crying that Christians blame him for everything. On a serious note, there are cults having satanic visitations where satan, who is their god, deceives them into thinking that he is the good one and God used him as a scapegoat. So you will see them use a symbol of the face of a goat with horns in a star in a circle, etc., which is supposed to be the scapegoat emblem to castigate God. All of these things are lies, whether it's posing as a joke or an occult practice.

There are many claims to the devil being a former archangel who rebelled in heaven and on and on and on. Well, I choose to believe the story of satan and his role from the beginning of creation as Jesus stated it. He said in John 8:44 that *the devil was a murderer from the beginning and the father of lies.* That is my conclusion and it is with this understanding that I keep the enemy out and subdued under my feet. In the story of Hannah, the Bible does not precisely indicate the presence of an enemy. In other words, there is no mention there of satan, the devil, demons, witches or witchcraft. And where it mentions the word evil, it is in reference to Eli's sons.

People from parts of the world where everything is seen as the enemy, the enemy, the enemy, will first and foremost conclude that it was the enemy that had Hannah barren. Without a doubt, someone can clearly state that perhaps, it was Hannah's mate, Peninnah, who went to a witchdoctor and closed up the womb of Hannah. He or she would explain that the reason for Peninnah doing this, if she did, would be because she wanted to gain greater favor with Elkanah, their husband by proving to him that she was his real wife since she was bearing children and Hannah was not. I'd say thank God that this suggestion has no grounds because that is not what happened. Folks have strange ways of thinking and always try to blame everything on the devil. I call them the lazy Christians. They refuse to take responsibility for what happens in their lives by blaming the devil for what goes wrong.

I remember a teaching I did once that had to do with the mind and the devil, in particular. It is titled, *The Carnal Mind is Death*. The message in it shows how our minds relate to demonic forces and gives strategies of how we should overcome them. I highly recommend that you get a copy if you don't have one.

The point I'm trying to make here by referring to the message is that people have said, "The enemy made me do it." So my question to them was, "Did you see the enemy appear to you and tell you to do whatever you said the enemy said you should do?" Obviously, it is clear that we do not see an enemy and sometimes this enemy that people are referring to is actually the carnal mind. Without the correct teaching on the enemy and the mind, it is quite easy to fall into a religious cliché that says 'it's the enemy'.

Thus, in the case of Hannah, where was the enemy? What happened that caused Hannah's womb to be shut? Who did it to her? Did she cause it to happen as a result of a past sin in her life? Was her barrenness a result of a curse?

I would quickly like to rule out those impressions, if any, that the enemy did this to Hannah. I would also like to point out that Peninnah had nothing to do with Hannah's barrenness. Neither was it some sin of Hannah's past or a family that led to her barren state. Breaking news! It was God. Yes indeed, it was God as noted in 1 Samuel 1:5 which reads, *"But on to Hannah he gave it worthy portion; for he loved Hannah: but the Lord had shut up her womb."* So it is quite clear Who did it.

God shut Hannah's womb so we have the answer as to who did it. We can also conclude from the previous Chapter that part of the reason for the barrenness was because of what God needed to be birthed in Israel. That was one aspect of her womb being closed. But could there have been other factors that led to God shutting her womb? Besides the destiny connection between she and Israel in light of the overall plan, does the Bible indirectly give us insight to something else that could have been another reason for her barrenness? Or rather put, was there an opening in Hannah's life that made it easier for barrenness to set in? The answer is yes, I will definitely expound on it in a later chapter. But for now, hold on to knowing that Hannah's barren state was well-connected with Israel's future of God birthing out the kingship realm of the nation.

Getting back to the enemy, as this Chapter indicates, is relevant because Hannah has to go past the enemy as well, regardless of whether he is to blame or not. When we are pursuing the destiny God designed for us, we will face situations, enemies, family pressures, our flesh and even religious systems. You should always perceive each aspect as obstacles that need overcoming. We are in God's School of the Spirit, being trained to think and act like God. If we are to be His Image, we must know how to reflect what He will do. This is the reason for His schooling. Thus, everything and everyone we encounter is on a direct or indirect mission of assisting us to succeed. Everything including the enemy.

Apostle Paul in II Corinthians 2:11 encourages believers to not be ignorant of the devil's devices; so that the enemy does not gain advantages over us. Ignorance, which is not knowing, can work against God's children by empowering the enemy. Satan will use the lack of knowledge as a cunning device to deceive and destroy. Therefore, becoming knowledgeable of what God says and how He says it, works to our advantage and disempowers the enemy. Satan's tools are only powerful against those who are not knowledgeable of God's Mind or walking in His Spirit.

Read what God says. *"My people are destroyed for lack of knowledge: because thou hast rejected knowledge, I will also reject thee..." (Hosea 4:6).* Our Heavenly Father's Words concerning ignorance are extremely disheartening. I pray that we as His Temple will move further into His All-Knowing Realm, and mature spiritually so as to avoid being victims of darkness.

In becoming familiar with the wiles of the enemy, know that the enemy will not always surface through people, and can remain very invisible. Spiritual warfare, as I mentioned earlier, is spiritual, which means that it is in another realm not visible to the physical eyes. Therefore, where can we accurately spot or find the enemy? That's right, in the spiritual realm. Searching for him there through the gift of discernment will lessen mistakes, and reduce the tendency of bringing false accusations against people that they are the enemy. Let's be very careful how we discern, because many have been victimized by it.

Satan is one term used to describe the enemy. The word means the opposer or adversary. He is always seeking someone to devour by influencing them to act as an opposing force. Here is what the Bible says in 1 Peter 5:8, *"Be sober, be vigilant; because your adversary the devil, as a roaring lion, walketh about, seeking whom he may devour:..."* The interpretation of this verse reveals that the enemy is not literally walking about like a physical lion roaring in search for people as food. No, using the functions and characteristics of the lion, and not it's physical form, will give understanding of what it means.

Hence, the verse implies that the adversary moves about spiritually, with fierceness and other brutal traits, similar to a lion in hunt for a prey. The enemy, like the lion, is also quite calculative prior to pouncing on its target. So we are warned by Apostle Peter in this verse to be sensitive and alert of the schemes and devices the enemy can use against us from the spiritual into the physical realm. Additionally, we are to know how the enemy sees us and what he wants to do to, and through us. Learning these things will vitally help your spiritual growth, keeping you from being used by darkness and being harmed by it also.

In Hannah's case, I would like to propose that the enemy was working threefold. Firstly, evil was definitely working in and through the sons of Eli. This meant that God needed to find a replacement for them after rendering their just punishment. Because of the amount of time it took for all this to come into fruition, Hannah had to remain in her state of barrenness. Remember, Hannah was clueless to the fact that her child was to replace Eli's household.

The enemy had to complete its evil works in and through Eli's sons before judgement could occur. Thus, in Hannah's condition, it is safe to say that the enemy was working behind the scene. Notwithstanding, all of this was in God's divine timetable, whether she knew it or not.

Secondly, the enemy was directly present in Hannah's life, and set rule over our heart. This was made evident in the Scriptures when her husband made inquiries as to why she was crying, not eating, and grieved. Her dissatisfaction was obvious and it overflowed to the point of bitterness.

Yes, I know Hannah was praying for a male child and probably walking in belief that someday God would answer her, but grief and bitterness are not signs of the fruit of the Spirit. They are the works of the flesh. The flesh realm is where satan governs through sin. The flesh is a total enemy of God and opposes the things of godliness.

Working as and through the flesh, that is our carnal and earthly nature, satan can fight against the Plan of God from being fulfilled in our lives when we allow it. He will project ungodly thoughts in order to produce ungodly actions. If we do not yield our members to the Lord, that is, submit all of who we are to God including our thoughts, the enemy will reign in those areas not submitted, and sit as lord over our lives.

Dating back to Hannah's battle, she was fighting an enemy who was within her, which came forth through her thoughts, words, and actions of sadness, bitterness, desperation, discontentment, and anger. These were direct manifestations of the enemy at work in Hannah. We will discuss it further in a later chapter.

So far, we have seen the enemy work in two ways; behind the scene of Hannah's situation as it related to Israel, and within her very being. The last place that we see the enemy and see it more clearly stated is in the labeling of Peninnah as her adversary. First Samuel 1:6 reads, *"And her adversary also provoked her sore, but to make her fret, because the Lord had shut up her womb."* Now, it is not written that satan was the one provoking her, but in my understanding of spiritual things, anyone who is used as an adversary is a representation of the devil himself.

As if Hannah did not have enough to deal with, here comes Peninnah with the assignment of being Hannah's personal adversary. How evil can a person be? Peninnah had children. Why could she not show compassion to the state Hannah was in? What would she have done if she was the one with a shut womb? I'm certain that she would have longed for a child just as Hannah was longing for hers, and would have expected some level of compassion no matter how little.

You see, the enemy will not show up with horns and a long black tail, holding a pitchfork to attack. Oh no. He will always look for that willing vessel who can be influenced by him to produce evil, which can stand as an opposing force to someone else's success. In this case, Peninnah was a perfect candidate to work in his demonic organization against Hannah. Neither of the two women knew what God would do with any child born in their household, but I strongly perceive that the kingdom of darkness was able to see a light shine from heaven towards Hannah, and therefore, did everything possible to work as a hindrance.

The role Peninnah played as an adversary really affected Hannah. It made her situation feel worse than it was, because such taunting acts can cause tremendous emotional torment. These were direct attacks against Hannah's soul and womanhood. And yet, Hannah had to go past the enemy. She had to move beyond where Peninnah wanted her to be emotionally. Hannah had to go beyond all negative reactions from her end towards Peninnah irrespective of what Peninnah did or said. Hannah had to go past all three schemes of the enemy.

Listen dear reader, if the enemy can get you in a place where you become bitter, or anything as such, about what is happening to you, then he has gained an upper hand against you. Satan knows that he cannot take you out of God's Perfect Will, so he tries to negatively influence you to get yourself out of divine destiny. This is why it's very important that we remain steadfast to God in prayers, believing that He will answer those who diligently seek Him. Hebrews 11:6 reads, *"But without faith it is impossible to please Him: for he that cometh to God must believe that He is, and that He is a rewarder of them that diligently seek Him."*

The work of the enemy is to deceive, mislead, and manipulate with lies. These lies can be believable, because they will consist of some form of truth in them. The voice of the enemy will always sound as if it is God speaking. We will have to discern that it is not, by learning the Word of God and depending on Holy Spirit.

When I say learning the Word of God, I am not referring to memorizing Scriptures, even though that is a good practice. Learning the Word of God, in this regards, is being taught by Holy Spirit to know the Scriptures, to comprehend how a Scripture will interpret another Scripture, so that it can be applied for discernment. Discerning for deception can be tricky because the intent of the enemy is to deceive, but with the help of the Holy Spirit, you can be guarded from lies.

All of what the enemy does is to get us into the realm of flesh. If he can accomplish his aim, then we will find ourselves operating under the control of flesh, which will make it impossible to be in right standing with God, pray as we ought, or receive answers to our prayers. He magnifies the situation in the mind of the one who is not sensitive to his devices, so that he or she can focus on everything else but God, and what God can do. In short, the enemy wants to hinder this person from experiencing changes towards divine destiny. May this not be you.

The devil is so wicked that he will use those closest to us, because they are familiar with our situation, and they matter more than a stranger. Not only that, he will find the ideal candidate who can play out the role flawlessly. For Hannah, Peninnah was the perfect vessel to act as the adversary. Using a neighbor down the street would not have mattered much to Hannah in the way Peninnah did.

Travel in your mind to the scene and try to picture the culture back then. Hannah and Peninnah lived together in the same place. And even if it was different houses, I'm certain that they were not miles apart. They were mates of the same husband, and therefore, one could not avoid the other. From the rising of the sun till dawn, Peninnah was there in Hannah's face and head. If she did not say anything to Hannah, the very appearance of her children spoke as a reminder to Hannah's barrenness.

The most ill thing about this situation was that Peninnah provoked Hannah as they went up to the House of the Lord to worship. How cold can a person be? One would assume that going to the Lord's House for worship is a place where love would be shown to one another. But not so in the eyes of Peninnah. Those travel times where probably the best times to torture Hannah.

I believe part of the reason that Peninnah did this during those worshipful moments was because it was then that Elkanah, their husband, would give Hannah a double portion. His actions in my mind could have driven Peninnah to further jealousy, and because she could not take it out on him, she took it out on Hannah.

Someone else might say that Elkanah was not to blame for Peninnah's treatments to Hannah; it could have been Hannah who was first unfair to Peninnah, which resulted in the adversary attacks she received. But regardless of the reason, nothing can justify being used by the devil or being labeled as an adversary. Moreover, if Hannah did not have fleshly issues within herself, whatever Peninnah did would not have been a torment. Let me explain what I mean by this.

Jesus says in John 14:30, *"Hereafter I will not talk much with you: for the prince of this world cometh, and hath nothing in me."* Putting it another way would read, the prince of this world has nothing in Me whenever he comes. Jesus could say what He said because He knew and understood the ways of the devil. He also understood how to triumph over the enemy.

For one to overcome, he or she will need to know how the devil operates. Furthermore, he or she will need to be free of what belongs to the enemy. In other words, you cannot overcome the enemy when you have within you what roots from evil and belongs to it. Jesus lived His life free of all forms of evil. In Him was life and truth; walking in the ways of God in his thoughts, actions, and words. Therefore, He indicated to His disciples that satan was coming but could not prevail against Him because there was nothing in Him that belonged to satan. By the grace of God, we all will one day freely say the exact words of Jesus, *"...the prince of this world cometh, and hath nothing in me."*

Unfortunately, this was not the case with Hannah. The enemy worked against her with such impact because there were things in her that belonged to him. What were those things? As I mentioned to you earlier, they included bitterness, grief, discontentment, jealousy and anger. If Hannah did not have any of these things in her especially bitterness, nothing Peninnah could have said would have moved Hannah. Her attitude would have been to ignore Peninnah, and enjoy her husband's favor while waiting on the Lord to give her, her heart's desire.

For this reason, Hannah had to be processed by the Lord. Otherwise, she would have not fitted well into His overall Plan, and the answer to prayers would have been soiled by the evil roots springing up from her. With the eyes of revelation, Hannah, not been processed by God, could have never stood as a *prophetess* and a handmaid in the birthing of what Israel needed.

Hannah had to go past the enemy at work in the priestly line of Israel, within herself, and through Peninnah. But did you know that the enemy sometimes works on God's behalf? Yes, He sure does and that's good news. I'm hoping that I do not lose you because of what I just said. In fact, let me say it again, the enemy sometimes works on God's behalf. Or, to put it a better way, the enemy works for God. Hmmm. I had to take a deep breath after getting that out.

There is a story in First Kings 22 that can clearly supports what I just said about the enemy working for God. You can read the whole Chapter but here are verses 19 – 23:-

> *And he said, Hear thou therefore the word of the Lord: I saw the Lord sitting on His throne, and all the host of heaven standing by Him on His right hand and on His left. And the Lord said, Who shall persuade Ahab, that he may go up and fall at Ramothgilead? And one said on this manner, and another said on that manner. And there came forth a spirit, and stood before the Lord, and said, I will persuade him. And the Lord said unto him, Wherewith? And he said, I will go forth, and I will be a lying spirit in the mouth of all his prophets. And He said, Thou shalt persuade him, and prevail also: go forth, and do so. Now therefore, behold, the Lord hath*

put a lying spirit in the mouth of all these thy prophets, and the Lord hath spoken evil concerning thee.

All things are made by God and come from God. Evil is no different according to Isaiah 45:7, *"I form the light, and create darkness: I make peace, and create evil: I the LORD do all these things."* And so, God will use whatever is necessary. God did not want Israel's king to be lied to; but the king wanted to hear lies. He was not seeking truth, and did not want to receive the truth when he heard it from the true prophet. Hence, he received lies from the false prophets.

This story is a perfect example of how we can learn the ways of God and the operations of the enemy. If you were able to read the entire story, you would have seen that God did try to warn that wicked king long in advance, but he was not prepared to follow the ways of God. He wanted to satisfy himself. He wanted to remain wicked. And God will not force anyone against his or her will. We will have to always choose whether to open ourselves to the truth of God's Word, or to the lies and deception of the enemy. The results we get will show where we yielded ourselves in submission.

Because people do not know how evil works, they become victims. Some might consider it natural to be angry or hurt. But these are all seeds of evil that can grow into a mighty harvest of demonic practices and lifestyles. They are the works of the flesh and Galatians 5:19-21 lists some as, *"Adultery, fornication, uncleanness, lasciviousness, idolatry, witchcraft, hatred, variance, emulations, wrath, strife, seditions, heresies, envyings, murders, drunkenness, revellings, and such like:"*

Holy Spirit is working actively to bring each person into the Kingdom of God through deliverance from the kingdom of darkness. Salvation, which is accepting Jesus Christ as personal Lord and Savior, is the first step, but the work has just begun. All believers will have to go through processes upon processes by God in order to kill the flesh and its works, so as to live unto the Lord. He is a Holy God, and each one of His children must abide in the Holiness of His Spirit. That's why the Bible says *we are born of the Spirit*. The Holy Spirit, that is, and not just any ordinary spirit.

I agree that the whole processing of God will not happen overnight, and neither will it happen within a few hours or days. It's a spiritual journey, and prayer is one of the means by which God can process us. Through prayers He can change our destinies, because He can pray His Mind for us by His Spirit in us. It may start off as an individual praying to God for something very desirous, but God can use that to lead the person through a time of regeneration.

This is what I believe took place in the life of Hannah. In her journey into the destiny of receiving a child, she became processed by God. And as you can see, the process included going past the enemy, as well as the situation she found herself. Now we can move on to the next Chapter that discusses the need to go past the family. I pray you are being blessed by the journey so far.

The Family

4

In this Chapter, we will focus on the family structure of Hannah, and the importance of moving beyond her family. But before any explanation as to why Hannah had to move beyond her family, I would like for you to see if there exists a reason for such a transition. This will help train your eyes when it comes to your own family, and what you may have to do so that you can move further into your destiny.

People will not progress in life if they do not take the time needed to search for obstacles and hindrances over and above the obvious. Certain things require a closer look to see beyond the surface before we can know if there exists a threat or danger. Our lives are very precious, and therefore, no stone can be left unturned.

Take termites for example. They can cause major damages to properties for years without being noticed. An individual who is not a professional in the field of pest control may never understand the damage termites have caused until the bills come for repairs. It will take trained eyes looking beyond the external structures to see how dangerous the termites have been to the property. The quicker they are noticed and exterminated, the less damage they will cause.

The use of termites is an extreme example to use when it comes to family. Nonetheless, the lesson of identifying them early by looking beyond the surface is what I want you to keep in mind for this chapter's understanding, and for your life when applicable. In fact, every area of our lives should be closely scrutinized and done so as often as possible.

Family can be sometimes difficult just thinking about certain peculiar family members. Unlike the enemy that operates in the unseen realm, family is very visible. Some family members are so visible that you sometimes think you're seeing yourself through their resemblance or actions. There are some that you wish were not a part of your family at all. Whilst, there are others that you love out of this world.

Regardless of our feelings as they develop over time about our family members, family is what we start with from birth, and what we end with. So, how does one go past their family when family, in most cases, has been there all along? Even more so, why should an individual have to go past their family or certain family members in particular?

It may seem like a difficult thing to do when you look at this on the surface. Actually, breaking past the family is very difficult. The individual in pursuit of the destiny God has for him or her will have to make very hard decisions. These decisions will affect not only the family, but also self. It will involve the heart; and when it comes to family, they are in the very center of our hearts and lives. Won't you agree?

I am certain that your mind, by now, is already giving ideas of decisions you might have to make when it comes to your family; be it immediate family, extended family, church family or any other entity you consider family. But before you charge out with your personal decisions, tune back to Hannah.

There is not much mentioned in the Bible about her family besides her husband. It does not provide any information about who her parents were, and we know that she had no children as of yet. Notwithstanding, much is presented to us for learning purposes and spiritual growth.

At first glance, it would look as though Peninnah and her children could be considered Hannah's immediate family since they were all of the same household. However, the few lines that describe the relationship between these two women do not leave room to say that Peninnah was one of Hannah's favorites, and neither does it present a picture of Hannah considering them as her family. Theoretically, we can say that they were all family. But, I believe that the bond of family, which is love, was not there, and if it was, it was buried.

I find this aspect of going past the family to be very essential to the journey that every one of us will have to take as we move towards destiny changes. For some, it will be a very easy thing to do. But to others, it can become so difficult that they are never able to break the soul-ties that are rooted deeply within the heart. Very heartbreaking it is to see people get stuck by family matters in light of Kingdom advancements. Consequently, prayers become dangerous rather than advantageous for the one who God is calling higher.

The deeper we go in prayer, the more engaged we become with the matters of the heart. Everything within the heart, and everyone, stands as either an asset or a deterrent. The higher we go in God, we find ourselves wanting God to be the absolute occupant of our hearts. We want Him to fill us completely, and that leaves room for almost no one else.

Moreover, we must learn how to position those that have a rightful place in our hearts far from where God occupies, His Throne. This is the throne of our hearts for we are His Temple. We should never exult anyone to that place of the highest authoritative voice in our lives. It belongs to God and God alone.

The high calling of God in Christ Jesus requires everything that we have and all of who we are. When we submit all to God, He then will exalt us as He did with Christ; not to be above Him, but to be with Him. This high call presents us with an opportunity to sit in the Throne of God in Christ Jesus according to Revelation 3:21, *"To him that overcometh will I grant to sit with me in my throne, even as I also overcame, and am set down with my Father in His throne."*

Anyone seeking to sit in the Throne of Jesus Christ in order to rule with Him, will have to sacrifice all, including the overcoming of family ties. Consider Jesus, our Pattern. He did not sacrifice His family, but being a sacrifice Himself, He had to separate

Himself from family. He had to guard His emotions, otherwise, He may not have made it to the cross, which was His ultimate sign of obedience to the Father.

Whilst on the cross, the disciple John, recorded a brief conversation between himself, Jesus and Jesus' mother, Mary. It's almost like an exchange was going on, a transference of responsibility that was filled with love, compassion, and vision. Jesus was taking transitional steps past His earthly family into His spiritual family.

His destiny was so purposeful that nothing could alter it or be a hindrance. This was part of the price He had to pay to fulfill His *High Call* in God. So to make it easy, or easier, He simply turned to Mary and beckoned her to cast her eyes upon the one who could replace Him as an earthly son. Likewise, He turned to the son, John, and told him to behold his mother, Mary.

I am purposefully using the term *earthly* because in certain Christian denominations, it is believed that Mary is the mother of God. This my beloved reader is an abomination in my opinion. God has no mother, and the role of Mary was for earthly purposes ***only***.

She being the mother of Jesus ended at the cross. In addition, she had to go through Jesus in order to get into Heaven making Him her God, Savior, Father, and Lord. Thus, we do not pray to Mary, and we are not to direct any kind of communication to her or through her. We respect and honor her, but we certainly do not worship her.

Jesus knew that Mary was hurting along with all the others who loved Him dearly while He hung on the cross. He understood the pain they felt from seeing Him so unjustly handled and wrongfully persecuted by men. If they could have had their way, they would have taken Jesus off the cross and hung His persecutors on it instead. To them, this would have been their expression of love. However, that was not the expression of love God wanted displayed.

Our Father in Heaven requires of us to have and show the kind of love that walks in absolute obedience to His Word. Nothing else should ever take His place in our lives. Again, no one or nothing is allowed to share God's Throne in our hearts. We are His Temple and He alone reigns if we say we are His.

Does that mean that there is no place in our hearts for families? Family members have their places, but they should not be given authority in our lives above God's authority. Simply put, we are not to obey any voice that could sound louder than God's. Our walk of obedience will show who sits in the highest place of our hearts.

In all things God comes first. He is Ultimate, Supreme, and Holy. There is a place for families, and each member should be kept in their place of positioning in our hearts. This step is important, because, if we do not take heed, we can become extremely attached to a member of our family including spouses. The attachment can become a spiritual rival against God's place. And if care is not taken, the enemy can use this to our disadvantage. This is where familiar spirits have field days of triumphs.

That is to say, they thrive on relationships that speak louder to us than the Voice of God. Demonic influences will work through our family members to gain spiritual dominance and control over our lives when we allow it. Thus, discernment of voices is key. And shortly, you will see how this appeared in Hannah's life, which could have been a deterrent to her receiving her answer to prayers.

No one can understand what you go through except God, and probably yourself to some degree. No matter the extent or magnitude of love a family member can have for you, that individual will never know the fullness of your destiny, nor how it will eventually unfold. Being human limits their love. In fact, there are times when their expressions of love toward us are typically influenced by our behavior and what we share with them. They will become protective when we show them that we are in danger. They will become our providers when they know we are in lack.

Family will do anything to make it easier for us so that we don't have to go through any pain or suffering. This is how family generally shows love, not realizing that without the pain, there may never be a destiny change. God, on the other hand, Who is the Head of our Spiritual Family, knows exactly how to love; which is quite different from man's ways of loving.

Hannah experienced a human's love that wanted to make everything right for her the way he knew best. I am referring to the love of her husband, Elkanah. *"Then said Elkanah her husband to her, Hannah, why weepest thou? and why eatest thou not? and why is thy heart grieved? am not I better to thee than ten sons?" (I Samuel 1:8).* In comparison to what Hannah needed, I could have responded on behalf for her to say, no Elkanah, you are not better to me than ten sons. Listen, he loved her dearly, and he also wanted his joyful wife back; not the woman who was grieving for children. He wanted to make it right for her, and inevitably for himself.

I don't believe there's a man alive who wants a grieving wife. So, her pain was his pain as well. And as any man would do, he wanted to fix the situation.

Elkanah wanted to make Hannah happy in any way he could so that she would no longer suffer as she was. Regrettably, he could not do anything else for Hannah except join her in prayer for a child, or give her a child. I think she wanted both. In fact, she probably wanted to forget the prayers and let him just give her a child. Get her pregnant and her warfare would end.

But that was not the case and in all fairness to him, I think Hannah knew that her barrenness was not Elkanah's fault. He had children and could obviously reproduce. There are some cases where the couple is childless and both are trying to figure out who's fault it might be. But in Hannah's case, it was obvious where the problem was.

How many times did he try to comfort her? What extent did he go through in order to bring her some form of joy and fulfillment? I'm sure that Elkanah would have done anything to make his wife, Hannah, pleased and happy. However, his efforts and attempts were to no avail.

His love was limited and so was his voice in her ears. Moreover, his actions of love were sorrowfully darkened each time Hannah found out that Peninnah was pregnant again, and she was not. His question to her of not being better than ten sons quickly got answered each time he produced another child by the other wife.

Honestly answer these questions: If a family member's love is limited when it comes to the fulfillment of God's destiny in your life, why allow their voice to speak louder than God's? Why consider what family says when they speak contrary to that which the Word of God declares? Has your love been blinded that you can no longer see past your family? Who have you allowed to directly share the throne of your heart where God belongs? Who is it in your family that you know you have to go past now that you understand that family can be a hindrance?

The Bible is flooded with examples of separations from families in order to embrace destinies. Men are told to leave their father and mother in order to cleave to their wives, Genesis 2:24. In I Kings 19, we read about the record of Elisha saying to Elijah, *"Let me, I pray thee, kiss my father and my mother, and then I will follow thee."* This was not for marriage to a woman but marriage to a spiritual leader in order to fulfill his spiritual call.

Mark 10:28-30 (AMP) provides this account for our admonition.

> *Peter started saying to Him, "Look, we have given up everything and followed You [becoming Your disciples and accepting You as Teacher*

> *and Lord]." Jesus said, "I assure you and most solemnly say to you, there is no one who has given up a house or brothers or sisters or mother or father or children or farms, for My sake and for the gospel's sake, who will not receive a hundred times as much now in the present age—houses and brothers and sisters and mothers and children and farms—along with persecutions; and in the age to come, eternal life.*

Frankly, there's nothing else so certain that amplifies that we must go past family. Apostle Paul says it this way in Philippians 3:11-12, *"Brethren, I count not myself to have apprehended: but this one thing I do, forgetting those things which are behind, and reaching forth unto those things which are before, I press toward the mark for the prize of the high calling of God in Christ Jesus."* Those things speak of family as well. But one's hands have to be empty so that he or she can grasp what is ahead. We have to free ourselves of all that occupies our lives and holds us back, including family ties.

Hannah had to go past her family. She had to go past Peninnah, which was not very easy to do since Peninnah brought her hurt. She had to go past Peninnah's children, because seeing the children evoked covetousness, lust, dissatisfaction, sadness, and jealousy. Hannah had to go past her husband, because his love was not enough to satisfy her needs.

His love of wanting to be better than ten sons said one thing to Hannah. Whereby, his duty to Peninnah that had her give birth to sons and daughters, instead of Hannah, said something different.

The person who reads this book, especially this Chapter, may disagree with me because of how I perceive the Hannah situation. Unfortunately, believers wear a mask over what they truly think in order to present a 'holier than thou' attitude. Some teachers of the Bible cast veils upon the Truth of God's Word, making it difficult to see God for Who He really is. They want to present Bible characters as great heroes without indicating their faults and weaknesses. But none of these actions will help anyone to achieve the high calling of God.

It will take people facing the Truth; believing and accepting it for what it really is, and then, the Truth can establish itself in believers' lives. We must get to the place where we understand that it takes God's Grace and Mercy for anything good to happen to us, in us, for us, and through us. Our human efforts can never make it into the divine things of God. It did not work for Hannah, and neither will it work for you and me. Hannah too made a statement in this regard in 1 Samuel 2:9 *"He will keep the feet of his saints, and the wicked shall be silent in darkness; for by strength shall no man prevail."*

There are many incidences in the Bible that portray to us the need to go past family in order to achieve God's purpose. And when we are not willing to do so, God will allow situations and circumstances to bring us to that place. The life of Joseph written in Genesis is another prime example of how situations and family moved him further into God's Plan.

Had it not been for his hateful brothers who sold him into slavery, Joseph would have never ascended to Pharaoh's throne; becoming the second man in power over Egypt and the surrounding regions. Had it not been for the wickedness shown to him by his brothers, Joseph would not have left his father's side. His family was all he knew, and he understood how much his father, Jacob, loved and depended on him. All in all, there was no apparent reason for Joseph to leave his birthplace and family.

God had revealed His Plan in dreams through symbols, but none of them accepted what God was saying, and neither did they comprehend what He wanted to do with the life of Joseph. They interpreted it negatively, which created feelings so evil that some of the brothers wanted to kill him. Joseph had to go past his brothers' envy and hatred, and move beyond his father's intense love. Shockingly, slave trade was the vehicle God used to lead him out and away from the family. In Truth, God did the separating.

Another Biblical character who experienced family separation orchestrated by God was Abraham. He definitely had to go past his family to reach his promised land. There was no way God could have established His covenant with Abraham, while he lived in his biological father's house as part of his household. There had to be a complete separation, even to the point of removing, Lot, the last male family member Abraham took with him as he journeyed. Lot, which means veil, had to be removed before Abraham could clearly see. I stated male because Sarah was Abraham's half-sister, although she was his wife as well. But when God spoke with Abraham as the Bible indicates, it was never in the presence of Sarah.

There are certain places in the heights of God's Spirit that we can only ascend to alone. No one is permitted to go with us, and thus, we cannot try to take people into places where they do not belong. Not only is it dangerous for them spiritually, it is damaging to our personal walk with the Lord. We will not be able to gain access into some places within the Heavenly Realms if we are not alone with God.

When He calls a man, He calls that person alone. Be it a male or female, each one of us receives our destinies alone. Yes, there are helpers and help mates to the vision God gives, but the vision is given to one individual, not to a couple, group, family, tribe or nation.

Hannah (regardless of if she recognized her role in Israel's future) knew that there was something she had to get. Elkanah already had children and continued to, so there was no way he could truly feel the void within Hannah. If she had kept herself in that place of Elkanah's words of comfort, her life would have been a deception, because she knew that there had to be more than who he wanted to be to her.

Yes, she was bitter and dissatisfied, but I appreciate the fact that she did not lie to herself. She pressed beyond her husband's voice and other acts of matrimonial love into what God, the Lover of her soul, alone could do. She went past her human family and went to her Heavenly Father. When she did, she went to her true Source, the only One who could intervene to make the impossible possible. Completing this step of her journey was remarkable, but it was not the end, because Hannah still had to go past the priest and her flesh.

As I end this Chapter, permit me to give you some comforting words for whenever you have to go past family, especially, the ones who are purposed to remain in your life. Going past family does not mean that you have to break all earthly communications and relations. There are times when God will give precise instructions to do so, and if that is ever your case, keep in mind that God knows what is best for you. This will require absolute trust in Him.

Going past family is more or less a spiritual thing with emotional implications. It is moving your focus from off man, and turning it towards God in order to grow into complete dependence on Him. It is moving from the earthly life into the spiritual life with God.

Here is a key point to those of you who are married. Hannah went past Elkanah, but she did not divorce or separate from him in marriage. Some believers may think that this is the way to fulfill God's purpose, but divorce is not the instruction for all married couples.

It is sometimes easier to do the Lord's work as a single person, but being married has its advantages in fulfilling God's Plan. Hannah remained married and needed to. She and Elkanah continued to live together as husband and wife with Peninnah still a part of the family.

Going past family is allowing God to break any and all soul ties with anyone, family or not, who keeps you down or hindered in your walk with Him. Truth is, we were not meant to have soul ties, that's carnal and can be very demonic. We are to be joined with the Lord as one Spirit. The soul gets put under the subjection of the Spirit.

Thus, married folks will have to always remember that Jesus is Lord in the marriage. Those who are parents must release the reins and allow God to take charge of their children's lives. Siblings should grow knowing that they are individuals no matter how attached they become to one another. It is God first, then family. This order should never change.

Your pursuit of God has to be more powerful than your love for family. Your commitment to Him is primary. You will be of more value to your family once you can successfully walk as God's family in absolute union with Him. This will give you more power to help those you love.

How beneficial is it if everyone in your family is stuck? It will take someone breaking out through the help of God to bring back deliverance for destiny changes. You can; and most likely, are the one to do so if only you believe.

The Priest

5

Hannah's advancement to destiny change is truly commendable so far. Her progressive steps forward is headed in the right direction. Having passed her situation and her family, Hannah is moving further into God's agenda. What is interesting is that she still does not know what lies ahead of her. She has no inclination of the Mind of God concerning herself and her womb. She is about to give birth to one of the greatest men Israel is yet to know, but as an ordinary Israelite, all she knew was that she wanted a child.

Having passed all the obstacles and torments she had gone through, Hannah did not know that she had to go past Eli, the priest. A person can think that hell will break loose in the family if they are in pursuit of God, but that individual ought to watch out and see what happens when he or she comes to the church, or should I say, the religious system that labels itself as the *church*.

God's true Church is a place of comfort and solutions, not mockery and insults. Church leaders are to help individuals find God, not ridicule them while they are in search of Him. Hannah was in the right posture of prayer. And thank God, the priest was not her God.

At I Am Precious International Harvest Ministries, we consider ourselves to be at Home when we meet at our place of worship. It is a Home because it provides what is needed for spiritual growth and various supports for living in the earth realm. It is more than a hospital for healing, more than a restaurant for eating, and more than a house where folks live. We are a Home, a spiritual abode where the children of God can fellowship with Father and each other in Jesus Christ by the Holy Spirit. This is how a *church* or ministry should be.

Now see what happens when Hannah goes into the Temple according to 1 Samuel Chapter 1.

> *Now it happened as she continued praying before the Lord, that Eli was watching her mouth. Hannah was speaking in her heart (mind); only her lips were moving, and her voice was not heard, so Eli [h]thought she was drunk. Eli said to her, "How long will you make yourself drunk? Get rid of your wine." But Hannah answered, "No, my lord, I am a woman with a despairing spirit. I have not been drinking wine or any intoxicating drink, but I have poured out my soul before the Lord. Do not regard your maidservant as a wicked and worthless woman, for I have spoken until now out of my great concern and [bitter] provocation.*

The King James Version mentions her saying in verse 16, *"Count not thine handmaid for a daughter of Belial:..."* I find this to be quite interesting since Chapter 2 verse 12 refers to Eli's sons as sons of Belial. This is because they did not know the Lord, but Hannah did know God. There's quite a bit I can say about it since the Spirit has given the authority to do so.

Here is Hannah pouring out her heart to God in prayer and supplication. She is desperately seeking God in the way she knew how. She was not ashamed to pray because she understood that the shame came only because of her barrenness. It would have remained if she did not pray. Devastatingly, Eli could not discern a woman in prayer to YHVH *(Yahweh)* from a woman displaying as a drunken daughter of an idol, Belial.

He was an aged man, but not too old to not discern the difference between those who were children of the devil, Belial, and those who were children of the Lord, Yahweh. With all due respect, Eli should have recognized what Hannah was doing. Perhaps, he could not because he had become too accustomed to the ways of the children of Belial; given that two of them lived in his household, his very own sons.

Leaders in the Church will have to inspect with caution, the lives of those who serve with them in ministry unto the Lord. Some might start well but may get off track somewhere along the way. The importance of them inspecting others is to ensure in the best way possible, that there is limited, if not, no defilement in the service they provide. And this does not exclude the leaders themselves.

It will sound as though I am harsh or hard with Eli's actions when I talk about Hannah and what she had to go through. Honestly, I am, and I am intentionally doing so simply because, if we as leaders do not rebuke the evil lurking within our own household, it will be impossible to discern evil from those the Lord brings to us for spiritual guidance and help. And even if we do discern it, how authoritative will we be in the realm of the spirit knowing that we tolerate and condone it? What we do not rebuke and set right will signify that we are a part of it.

Eli had received warnings from the Lord about his sons and the evil they did in the Temple. Not only was he aware of it because it was obvious and the whole nation knew about it, but God directly told him. God instructed him to get it right. And what did he do? He talked to them about it, indicating that there was no one to intervene on their behalf since they were sinning against the Lord. Really?

Some may say that Eli did the best he could as a parent. After all the boys were men, not teenagers and young kids. But you see, when it comes to the priestly office, every priest is subjected to the high priest and in those days, it was Eli. I expected Eli to do more than just talk.

Their evil doings were not something that had just started when he had that conversation which is recorded later in Chapter 2 of 1st Samuel. Oh no, their acts of evil had been going on long before then. Season after season and year after year, they continued in disobedience to the Lord. Their disobedience grew and surmounted to the place where the Lord's judgment of death was upon them.

They knew they were in rebellion to Yahweh's Laws of priestly service, and with deception establishing itself as if all was well with them, they continued with no repentance whatsoever. By then, it was too late for Eli's warnings. Their hearts were hard, and our Holy God wanted them out of His sight. It was His Holiness that would have consumed them long before, but mercy and other parts of the puzzle had to be in place first.

What made it even more difficult for them to repent was that Hannah had prayed. Her child was the *better neighbor* in place of those worthless sons of Eli. Somebody was praying, and although Hannah was praying for herself, she was indirectly praying for Israel; because what she carried was the answer Israel needed. And God heard her, but not until she went past Eli.

When we leave the kingdom of darkness and are delivered into the kingdom of God's Light, which is revelation knowledge and experience of who God is, we must go past the priest. In other words, we must overcome the religious systems and false doctrines within the church realm. If not, we will never reach where God wants us to go.

So-called "servants" of God have become stars and idols. They set themselves up to be bigger than life. This blinds the people from seeing God, and therefore the sheep cannot be touched by God as they desire and as God desires to touch and heal them. These so-called priests of today are posing as gods, but have no power of godliness. Unfortunately, people continue to go to them week after week without receiving real answers. There is no power. God is not present there.

Many are reciting words, but have no Eternal effect. Philosophy is being taught and false doctrines are being formulated. They are building kingdoms, but none are of the Kingdom of God. Their institutions have dead creeds, lifeless confessional, and powerless rituals. They are man-made edifices, and *white-washed sepulchers* as Jesus once said. Fortunately, God is bringing in the true Church of His Son, and creation will see the manifestations of the sons of God very soon.

Our ministry is one of the few in the world that God is raising up according to the Pattern of Jesus Christ. I make this boast in HIM. The Statements of Faith of I Am Precious International Ministries come from the messages given by the Spirit of God to the churches in the Book of Revelation. There are seven churches and each one of them is instructed to overcome.

Seven church means the complete church realm, not just seven individual and geographical church buildings. We are the church, not the building we gather in nor the places we meet for fellowship. Thus, we must go beyond everything that stands as an obstacle within the church realm, and overcome; especially those that are hirelings and not true servants of God.

Below are our Statements of Faith. I pray that you will take these overcoming messages as your personal faith confessions. Moreover, incorporate them as your canon of things you're believing God for to happen in your life.

- Revelation 2:1-7 - *We believe in Him Who holds the seven stars in His right hand and walks among the seven golden lamp-stands. We believe that by overcoming, we have right to eat from the tree of life, which is in the paradise of God.*
- Revelation 2:8-11 - *We believe in Him Who is the First and the Last, Who died and came to life again. We believe that by overcoming, we will not be hurt at all by the second death.*
- Revelation 2:12-17 - *We believe in Him Who has the sharp, double-edged sword. We believe by overcoming, He gives us some of the hidden manna. We believe that He also gives us a white*

stone with a new name written on it, known only to us who receive it.

- Revelation 2:18-29 - *We believe in the words of the Son of God, Whose eyes are like blazing fire and Whose feet are like burnished bronze. We believe that by overcoming, He gives us authority over the nations. We believe that He also gives us the morning star.*

- Revelation 3:1-6 - *We believe in Him Who holds the Seven Spirits of God and the seven stars. We believe that by overcoming, we walk with Him in righteousness. We believe that He will never blot out our names from the book of life, but acknowledges us before our Father and His angels.*

- Revelation 3:7-13 - *We believe in Him who is Holy and True, Who holds the Key of David. What He opens no one can shut, and what He shuts no one can open. We believe that by overcoming, He keeps us from trails to test the inhabitants of the earth. We believe that He makes us pillars in the Temple of our God, never to leave again. We believe that He writes on us the Name of our God and the Name of the City of our God, the New Jerusalem; and He writes on us His new Name.*

- Revelation 3:14-22 - *We believe in the words of the Amen, the Faithful and True Witness, the Ruler of God's creation. We believe that by overcoming, He gives the right to sit with Him on His Throne, just as He was victorious and sat down with our Father on His Throne.*

These Statements are quite different from what most churches and ministry organizations have as statements of faith. For we at IAP Harvest, it is all about God apprehending us into His Mind and Purpose. Yes, we do believe in everything the Bible says, and not simply beliefs of what has happened. We want to have present faith with action. We choose to believe that God will manifest in us all He desires as our destinies. Not the destinies we want, but the destinies He planned and indicated in His Word.

So believing, for example, that Jesus was born of a virgin is good and true. But how is that a statement of faith? How does that relate to faith and works, since faith without works is dead? What more is there to believe for once you come to know that Jesus was born of a virgin? Knowing this establishes truth in you, but what does it mean to you and what can that knowledge do for you in the *now*? Our walk in the Lord is active. That's why it's called a walk, we have to move forward and keep making progressive steps in Him and with Him. Thus, we make Statements of *Faith*.

Hannah was doing just this when she stepped into the Temple to pray. Her prayers signified her forward movement into God. Apparently, Eli was not moving anywhere. No wonder Hannah was going past him.

In fact, the Bible records him sitting on a seat by a post of the Temple. There's a reason why the Bible registers that fact. The high priest had a seat of judgment where people came to meet him for advice and justice. But somehow, his judgment of Hannah's actions were very much off key. He judged her wrong, and if she was not a woman of purpose, his judgment could have distracted her and gotten her off track.

Instead of sitting on the seat to pass judgment on Hannah, he should have been rendering just punishment to his sons for their evil actions. Plainly put, he should have sentenced them to death by stoning. Oh yes, they were worthy of death, and Eli should have been the one to do so as high priest.

It appeared that he too needed to go past his family, and break the soul ties he had with his sinful sons; so that he could have been pleasing to God. I'd rather be alone in my walk with God righteously, than to mingle with mixed multitude of personalities whose ways are displeasing unto Yahweh. There can be no compromise whatsoever.

Was Eli sinning? Not according to the law; but in righteousness, he was a part of their sins, since he did nothing about it. Was it not Aaron, Moses' brother and the first high priest of Israel, whose sons got killed by God? Yes, and it is recorded in the Book of Leviticus 10: 1-3.

> *And Nadab and Abihu, the sons of Aaron, took either of them his censer, and put fire therein, and put incense thereon, and offered strange fire before the Lord, which He commanded them not. And there went out fire from the Lord, and devoured them, and they died before the Lord. Then Moses said unto Aaron, This is it that the Lord spake, saying, I will be sanctified in them that come nigh Me, and before all the people I will be glorified. And Aaron held his peace.*

Did you read that? They got burned for offering up strange fire while on duty. But their death also was not something that suddenly happened merely because of one incident. If you study the books of Leviticus and Numbers, you will see that there were several things clearly indicated as sins of these priests, Aaron's sons. They did not do what was commanded of them while in service:- they offered strange fire which meant that it was of their own accord and not the fire of the altar as the Lord instructed; they had the wrong timing of offering incense; they failed to sanctify themselves; and got drunk during holy services.

I am not sure what Aaron did about the sins of his sons prior to them dying, but I do know that there was nothing he could say or do about it after their death, except to obey the ongoing instructions of Moses. I do believe that Aaron was aware of their wrongdoings, and I also want to believe that God had given warnings prior.

God is Holy and His works are Perfect, but He uses imperfect people to accomplish His purposes. I've also learned from Apostle Asibor that God will change the individuals if He has to, but He will not change His Plan. It is always best to be in your rightful place of service. Do not have someone else take your place because God has to replace you. Disobedience and willful sinning are sure to guarantee a removal from the Plan of God if there is no repentance.

May that not be your portion.

The Flesh

6

Who Hannah was and who she became is amazing. Her story is one of hope and tremendous insight into the ways of God through the power of prayer. She was able to reach a destiny she had not imagined was possible for her. Hannah's desire was a small thing to God, but to her, it seemed like forever to get it fulfilled. For the most part, that's how it will appear in man's eyes, but God's timing is never too long.

Hannah's journey into destiny changes has taken her from a deep place of want to facing strong oppositions and adversaries. Not willingly but necessarily, she had to go past her situation, her enemies, family and her priests. Who would have thought that receiving an answer to prayers was going to stir up all that warfare? And, who would have thought that it would take as long as it did for an answer?

We are in a generation of speed and everything should be done quickly it seems. Fast food, fast apps, fast marriage ceremonies, fast cars, quick cash, and on and on and on. Waiting is like an international curse that has plagued our world. Who wants to wait? And for this reason, some think and act as if God is a magician that answers when they touch their magical wands. But let me tell you a secret: He's NOT.

We work on God's time, and we are to practice waiting on Him, because we are the ones needing to fit into His Agenda and not the other way around. This is something Hannah discovered and the discovery was painful. It took multiple journeys to the Temple, days and nights of tears, and probably wavering faith, just to name a few. What have you believed God for that hasn't happened yet, and you feel that you've prayed enough and for too long? The answer is coming once it is in His Will.

Have you heard of Zachariah, John the Baptist's father, who along with his wife, Elizabeth, waited years for a child? The account of their story is in Luke 1:5-25. They had waited so long that I think he forgot he even prayed for a child. Sometimes we forget but our gracious God will never fail to remember what we have need of. He did not forget this couple either, but like Hannah's scenario, they had to wait because their child was in God's Perfect Will. Hence, everything had to go according to Heaven's Plan. Just like your life if you belong to Him.

Zachariah had so forgotten that when angel Gabriel showed up to announce the answer, Zachariah was in doubt. Of course, part of the reason was because he and Elizabeth had given up on their bodies being capable of producing children. Read how he responded to the good news from the angel in Luke 1:18-20 (AMP).

> *And Zacharias said to the angel, "How will I be certain of this? For I am an old man and my wife is advanced in age." The angel replied and said to him, "I am Gabriel; I stand and minister in the [very] presence of God, and I have been sent [by Him] to speak to you and to bring you this good news. Listen carefully, you will be continually silent and unable to speak until the day when these things take place, because you did not believe what I told you; but my words will be fulfilled at their proper time.*

And so it was that the father to be was made dumb until the naming of his son, John. When reading the story, one can't help but feel sorry for Zachariah, but that is what happens when the flesh gets in the way. His mouth declared his doubt and the timing of it was just wrong. How could he doubt what God wanted to do, especially through the means He chose to deliver the message?

What was needed to secure the surety of receiving their answer was done; and that was to shut Zachariah up. His words were weighty, particularly being that he was a faithful priest. Thus, there could be no interference in the spiritual realms of what God was doing. Our words have power and can add to or hinder our prayers. Silence your flesh, and speak wisely.

Zachariah received mercy and got help with his flesh, the aspect of unbelief spoken from his heart through his mouth, but what was manifesting from Hannah's flesh? Remember that, when I speak of flesh, I'm referring to the carnal or base nature, mind and ways of mere men; immature believers. Acts of the flesh are humanistic behaviors caused by darkened thoughts as a result of being far from God. Such thoughts lack the guidance of the Word of God and His Spirit. Yahweh said in Isaiah 55:8, *"For My thoughts are not your thoughts, neither are your ways My ways, saith the LORD"*.

Did Hannah have fleshly issues that had to be dealt with? Obviously she did, and I will focus on one that has enormous and detrimental effects in people's lives if not dealt with by God. It is the root of bitterness. So let's talk about it for a while for better understanding of what had to occur in Hannah's life prior to her giving birth. And not just having a baby, but what was necessary to put her in readiness to stand for the generations to follow.

The Root of Bitterness

This root is poisonous and can hinder, delay, sabotage, and even cause a destiny to be aborted. Unfortunately, many are not aware of it. They do not know that it exists deep in their heart until God shines light on it.

There is no way to emphasize that the root of bitterness can seriously defile a person. It can corrupt the believer's state of holiness. It can hinder a person's walk in the Light of God's Word. It can stop people from moving forward in God.

The root of bitterness is in both believers and unbelievers. People often enter with it into the

Kingdom of God. In other circumstances, it develops when the believer is not getting rooted in Christ after becoming born-again. Thus, Colossians 2:6-7 states, *"As ye have therefore received Christ Jesus the Lord, so walk ye in Him: Rooted and built up in Him, and established in the faith, as ye have been taught, abounding therein with thanksgiving."*

In Ephesians 3:17-19, it reads, *"That Christ may dwell in your hearts by faith; that ye, being rooted and grounded in love, May be able to comprehend with all saints what is the breadth, and length, and depth, and height; And to know the love of Christ, which passeth knowledge, that ye might be filled with all the fullness of God."*

There must be a constant growth process taking place with righteous roots growing downward in the Word, and fruits of the Spirit upwards. However, if the roots are of a difference kind which is fleshly or carnal, it will either bear no fruit or bear ungodly fruits. One of such kinds is this root of bitterness. Hannah, in my opinion, had this kind of root. If it was not in her bloodline, she became opened to it somewhere during her dilemma of barrenness, and it grew.

To better comprehend this, let us define roots. In understanding spiritual things, we know that we look at the functionality of the symbol used, and not just the form of it. Roots as a symbolic word are parts of a plant that attach themselves to soils or other exteriors for support; and to provide what the plant needs like water and nutrients for growth. Applying this as a symbol to believers is appropriate, because we are like trees according to what the Bible teaches.

Christ is symbolized as the Tree of Life. He declared in John 15 that *He is the vine and we are the branches*. David in Psalm 1 proclaimed that a blessed man, *"...shall be like a tree planted by the rivers of water, that bringeth forth his fruit in his season; his leaf also shall not wither; and whatsoever he doeth shall prosper."* So having roots is very natural for all believers in Christ, since we are symbolized as trees.

Spiritually, roots are connections such as certain thoughts, imaginations, and feelings within a person that connect them to the spiritual realm. However, they are problematic when they are bitter roots. Hebrew 12:15 says, *"Looking diligently lest any man fail of the grace of God; lest any root of bitterness springing up trouble you, and thereby many be defiled;"*

Having roots in itself is not bad, and is rather encouraged to have for spiritual growth in God. But when one is connected to the spiritual realm with their roots, which spirit entity is he or she connecting to? Or, what kind of spirits is the individual giving access to? Is it one of the Seven Spirits of God, or demonic legions? Is the connection soulish or spiritual in nature?

Considering these questions is relevant for every believer, because the spirit is what energizes the vessels. Humans are vessels or bodies filled by spirits. When the Holy Spirit does not have fullness of the believer or full possession, other spirits move in if they were not already there. A individual can either be Holy Spirit filled, demonically possessed, or host a mixture of spirits. Only the first filling is good.

The role of our roots are to connect us to a source for support and sustenance. They are to connect to God alone as Source, but sometimes, Christians get or remain connected to other sources. It is our responsibility to check the roots' existence and growth by continually bringing ourselves into submission to God for healing, deliverance, and pruning. Only He can kill something as deadly as the root of bitterness if present, and forewarn us of their possible future appearance. When such root is not killed and plucked up, it will lay dormant for a season, only to spring up again when it finds an opportunity to express its wicked self. As long as the root is there, it will do what it does, attach and transport.

Now, notice that I speak of the root of bitterness, which is more than just being connected to bitterness or other evil sources. The root itself is bitter and a product of bitterness. It must be destroyed, and never permitted to grow. It feeds from the source of bitterness, and releases bitter sap; causing a person to be barren, or produce bitter fruits in life.

Strong's Concordance defines bitterness as *extreme wickedness, bitter hatred, harsh, virulent*. When Hannah confesses that she was in bitterness of soul, what exactly did she mean? It can only imply that she was bitter in emotions, feelings, and attitude. She had bitter emotions, thoughts, feelings and attitude. With this in mind, how could she have ever expected to receive from the Lord?

When the root is evil, the fruit will be evil likewise. Being bitter is like being poisoned and don't know what caused it. The bitter person finds every reason to justify why he or she should feel that way. It is always someone else's fault.

When bitterness sets in, it deceives its victim and causes them to feel unjustly treated. They begin to interpret situations as though they are entitled to special treatments, certain recognitions, various levels of appreciation, etc. Consequently, when things do not go the way they expected, the root of bitterness releases its sap as rejection, victimization, pity, offense, and other similar traits.

Furthermore, it projects itself within the environment to pollute it and others. It starts to manifest, and the poisoned carrier changes to reflect its evil face of bitterness. What appeared to be a good natured person is now acting sour and malicious. Whoever is the reason for not granting him or her what was thought to be an entitlement is hated and despised.

Those who are discerning can spot activities of the roots of bitterness within the flock, family, and among friends and associates. For illustration, let's say Marikale is a faithful attendant in church; she tithes and is always giving in support of the work of ministry. But if her givings are not done by obedience to God, the root of bitterness can surely set in. When others come along and do similarly as led by God, Marikale will begin to feel as if there is a mistreatment happening to her; because others are being recognized and appreciated, and not her. She is no longer in the spotlight, so she grieves.

She will begin to grumble within about how much she has given, and how much she has done. Later, her thoughts will become audible as she shares them with others in a spiteful and indirect way. She will look for audiences that are susceptible to gossip and undermining talk of the leader. Not only is Marikale infected by this root, she is now a toxin to the spiritual atmosphere in general. Even worse, is that she still thinks she is justified by her actions in spitting out venom.

She forgot when she claimed that her works were unto the Lord, and not the leader. Marikale may have started off well, but somewhere along the journey, she stumbled by offense. An underlying thought was taking root to cause her to think that her good works were gaining her favor. And when she was no longer the highlight of things, she exploded with bitterness. The root sprung up to troubled her first, and later, those around her. At this point, only deliverance from the root of bitterness can free Marikale and restore her.

In IAP Intl. Harvest Ministries, we fight to keep the root of bitterness out of our midst. It is clear that no one is entitled to anything, or any position, if God does not instruct it that way. Moreover, there has to be a continual growth in the Word with Spirit-filled applications to stay in a position. Revelation and illumination are God's requirements to us for receiving and maintaining stewardship positions of authority. It is about obtaining and sustaining holiness in our midst so that He can flow freely among us to create the Glory.

Likewise, God's Plan was for holiness to reign in the priesthood of Israel, and therefore, Hannah's childbearing had to be of a pure and holy root. She had to go past her flesh by conquering it through prayers. Thus, the Bible records her explaining to Eli that she was pouring out her soul to the Lord. A soul of bitterness is the consequence of a heart of bitterness, and God wants us to pay very close attention to it through the account of Hannah.

She poured out her soul. This was the remedy needed and prayer took her there; to that place of naked confession to God. She realized what her problem was and saw how it had become a major obstacle in her life. What started as an innocent and natural desire for a child was used by the enemy to corrupt Hannah's soul up to a point that she was mistaken to be a drunken idol worshipper. It was from out of the abundance of her heart that her mouth released inaudible words, yet, weighty enough to draw attention.

I believe that Hannah's soul was extremely bitter, and partly for that reason, she could not conceive until she encountered God for the dealings of her flesh. Yes, she was in God's process of timing relating to Israel, but in conjunction to that, Hannah was not going to give birth until she was set free of her internal torments. She was not permitted to bring forth God's choice with a heart of bitterness.

God shut her womb, and it was not only because she was included in His Plan. Hannah was also not walking in the Spirit. She was fleshly, and flesh can never birth things that are spiritually inclined. A transformation of heart and soul had to occur. Jesus says in John 3:6, *"That which is born of the flesh is flesh; and that which is born of the Spirit is spirit."* Hannah was to give birth to a spiritual plan of God, so He had to kill that root of bitterness in her flesh.

It affected her both spiritually and physically. In the physical, Elkanah was having sexual intercourse with Hannah, but the root of bitterness was pushing back conception. If she found it difficult to receive his love, how could she have received his child? He said, *"Am I not more to you than ten sons?"* But Hannah could not receive that expression of love; not even the double portions he served her.

Indeed, he could not give her what only God could supply, but her attitude towards him was wrong. She had lost her sense of intimacy, something very much needed before conception can happen at times. Hannah had narrowed down marriage to a child and could not see past it. She had allowed bitterness to consume the whole of her being. This root had grown deep and was bearing much fruitage of death.

It is not what happens to us that God judges us for, but rather, how we respond. Hannah had to stay strong in faith as she prayed, so she is not judged for that. She is judged for the other things she allowed to spring up and defile her while she prayed and believed. The Bible does not say that Hannah was behaving wickedly to others, but it does not have to before one can see that her thoughts were just as darkened as her unrevealed actions. People may think that it is alright to think it just as long as they do not act out what they think. That mindset is vile. *"As a man thinks in his heart, so is he" (Proverbs 23:7)*

God Who searches the very intentions of the heart will have to purify the vessel so that it is consecrated unto Him for His use. It has to be holy. Holiness in manifestation is an outpouring of sanctification in being and nature. Our Heavenly Father is concerned about what we become, and not merely what He can do through us. He works deep within so that our fruits are glorifying to Him, and eternally benefiting to us. Hannah was one of those blessed to be chosen for such a work of the Master.

Everything not rooted and grounded in Him must die. All forms of bitterness must leave especially if a person is about to give birth to what God desires. It becomes a product of God, and God is not going to release or allow conception in the midst of all kinds of roots that do not connect to Him. God by obligation to Himself has to get rid of defiling things within our being.

I highly value what Jesus said towards the close of His earthly assignment in John 14:30, *"Hereafter I will not talk much with you: for the prince of this world cometh, and hath nothing in me."* I love His statement of truth, and I am constantly putting myself in the position to say the same. Which means that there should be nothing in me that satan can communicate with. One day soon, it will be known that there is nothing in me reflecting the devil's image. There is nothing in my flesh that he can use and penetrate through. There is no root in me that can connect with him. I am free of all forms of bitterness. Do you believe the same for yourself? Well, you should.

It's time to release to the devil all that belongs to him, every root, stem, sap and fruit. We are of a different soil and different Source. We are of God in Christ Jesus. Hence in this process, we will find Father God always allows situations to come about to check our roots. There will always be tests to see how we will respond and what will be released from within us. There will always be things that take place for you, in you, and around you to see which spirit you've connected to and has gained access to you. It is always about the spiritual.

Hannah was on a spiritual journey and her roots had to be right. She was connecting to sources that caused her to be provoked by her mate. Peninnah's taunts could identify with something in Hannah and trigger fleshly reactions. Hannah would not have been moved if there was nothing in her for evil to attach itself to. The enemy was used to show Hannah things in her that were not worth having around when seeking the Face of God for a change in destiny.

You are on your personal journey to change destiny. What's your connections? Are they serpentine or divine? Are they allowing you to give birth in prayers to the things of God? Whether you are sure or unsure, pour out your soul to God and let Him be your Judge. Don't give room to satan to point out things that belong to him in you. Fully release yourself to God.

If the root of bitterness is in you, be truthful with God and say that it has not left, because every time you see the person who hurt you or you assumed hurt you, you're tormented. Every time you remember the situation something moves you negatively. Or perhaps, every time you want to give, you consider what happened to you the last time when they took advantage of you.

Every time you want to move forward in God, you experience something else happening that is contrary. Whatever Holy Spirit is putting His Finger on in your life, be truthful to God about it and allow Him to work. More often than ever, the root of bitterness is the underlying cause of all these things.

Now, it will be a little more difficult if the root produces anger towards God and unforgiveness. This root is quite capable to doing so. People with bitter roots are prone to becoming angry with God and blame Him for the negative things that happen to them. In their minds, God has all power to do all things, so why did He not act according to how they assumed He should have. Unfortunately, for them, they do not know God by principles and neither do they know His ways. They are in need of encountering His Love.

It is in the absence of these encounters with God that they become bitter towards Him. How then can they be opened to His Hand of healing and deliverance? How would they be able to submit to His processing?

Many fall short in the processing journey of prayer, and are far from being reached by God. Notwithstanding, there is the factor of the prodigal son who can return when he or she remembers the truth about the Heavenly Father. There is always hope for the poisonous spread of the root of bitterness.

Hannah received this hope because she received a touch from God that transformed her heart and soul. When you see later who Hannah became, you will learn of how everything about Hannah changed, including her purpose. She was not an evil woman, but the root of bitterness conquered her. Thank God for the application of prayer, and its power to transform as it works out the receiving of answers to the requests it bears. Hannah truly began to live out who she was purposed to be all along. But, it did not happen until she received relief from the root of bitterness. Not until she went past her flesh to be able to see God.

Her eyes were opened during her healing, as she prayed that faithful day in the Temple. After pouring out the bitterness of her soul in full, she began to release divinity. It's not that Hannah's answers were not right there with her; it's just that she was blinded to it. Because, she allowed evil to dictate to her sight. It was a dark covering clouding her vision, and only prayers could grant her deliverance. God killed Hannah's fleshly nature to allow her to see a much bigger, and higher purpose, His. It was no longer about her, but all about Him. She realized that she was only a benefactor in the equation if she walked in agreement with Yahweh.

What a blessed end for Hannah! I pray the same is yours at the end of your journey of prayer when you move past yourself, and your flesh.

The Meeting

7

It's a big day in the life of Hannah, and all of Heaven is rejoicing because of what God is about to do. To Hannah, it is another day of the year that she goes into the Temple to pray. She is not sure of what the results will be this time, and probably wavers a little in faith that there will be a change to her barren state. Anyhow, she continues the journey that has now led her to the meeting with none other, but God.

No, she did not go to meet with Eli. He had nothing really to do with her at this point, and there was not much he could do about changing her situation from barrenness to fruitfulness. This was a one-on-one with God, and nothing was going to stop her regardless of the answers she would have left with. Of course, to Hannah, it would be awesome if the answer was an immediate yes and amen; but if not, I'm quite certain that she would have returned for another meeting.

You see my beloved reader, sometimes it only takes one encounter to change and establish what God wants to do in and with us. Just one! Although, we sometimes will not know for certain if the next one will be the ultimate one. We respond with faith to the best of our abilities, but unfortunately, somewhere inside could lurk a slight 'what if' of doubt.

Disappointments of it not happening before, when we believed effortlessly, is the cause of this hidden doubt of it ever happening no matter how strong in faith we think we are. For moments like these, there is always a close Friend to turn to Who will comfort us with His Presence. He is none other than Holy Spirit. He knows how to handle all doubts. Moreover, when and if we do not know how to pour out our soul during a meeting with God, Holy Spirit does the praying for us. The apostle Paul in Romans 8:26 puts it this way, *"Likewise the Spirit also helpeth our infirmities: for we know not what we should pray for as we ought: but the Spirit itself maketh intercession for us with groanings which cannot be uttered."* **What a lovely God!**

Beloved, in light of this, there is one thing to hold for certain when meeting with God. That is, He will always be there. Sometimes, He's there before we arrive. After all, is it not His Temple? He will be there whenever He sees fit. Fortunately, for Hannah, this is how it was when she arrived on that faithful day. The Glory had not yet departed from the Temple, gratefully. Because, the high priest was there but could not do much. His sons were around somewhere sinning. Besides, they were definitely of no help to Hannah. But regardless of who was there or not there, who could help or not assist, Hannah had God, and He was there waiting for her arrival.

There was not much protocol for Hannah to follow except for being able to pray. Or should I say, pour out her bitter soul and anything else she had purposed to say. Some may think that praying is hard, but it's not, when understood that it is simply pouring out one's soul to God in all truthfulness and fervency; irrespective of the state or condition the soul is in. The essential ingredient needed is believing that God hears, and will answer. Thus, she seemed quite prepared for this meeting and did what was expected. Hannah PRAYED.

Praying is not difficult at all. Yes, there are times when certain prayer knowledge and strategies will make a huge difference in the act, but praying is quite simple. It's what all believers ought to know to do. A person starts their Christian life with prayers. That is how we got born-again. We prayed what we had come to believe by the help and leading of Holy Spirit.

I have a manuscript soon to be published on prayer, and how one can become an expert at it. You see, it's about getting the foundation and basic guidelines in place. I'll share a bit here with you, because it is that simple. Hannah did not have written strategies to follow, nor steps of prayer she prior studied. No, she had her soul, desire, and honesty. She knew the basics.

Prayer is a form of communication between an individual and the supernatural realm:- in our case, the supernatural realm is God. We do not pray to any other entity in the spirit world but God, not Mary, angels, or past saints. We pray to God our Father in Jesus Christ by the Holy Spirit.

The focus of this point is to know that ***prayer is a form of communication.*** It implies that you should learn how to communicate properly, in order to be effective in your praying. Not by diction eloquence or the use of technical language, but by fervency in your expression of what you desire to tell God. In addition, one does not need to be repetitious which sometimes is an attempt to lengthen the time of prayer. Repetitive prayers will not make anyone appear as a powerful prayer individual, if that's the intention. Such lengthy prayers are meaningless. Jesus said in Matthew 6:7-8, *"And when you pray, do not use meaningless repetition as the Gentiles do, for they think they will be heard because of their many words. So do not be like them [praying as they do]; for your Father knows what you need before you ask Him."*

Prayer is simply communicating with God about your desires so that you can have favorable results. Once the heart has spoken and released all the cares of the soul, that is it. There's nothing else to say, just wait for Him to respond. We have presented ourselves to Him, hiding nothing and giving no room to pretense. We realize that He cares for us and loves us in spite of our weaknesses and shortcomings.

Some might say that God knows everything so why communicate with Him. Well, once we realize and accept that prayer is an opportunity for communion and/or communication, we will not hesitate to dialogue with Him about all that concerns us. And He enjoys us doing so.

During one of our Thursday Mentoring Sessions, we looked at understanding *form* verses *function* of symbols. I instructed each person to give descriptions of what prayer can symbolize based on its functionality. It was interesting to see how the mind will provide insight once it is attentive and directed to the Holy Spirit for input. After those being mentored shared what they came up with, I provided them with mine. Below is the list of what prayer can be and do, depending on how one views it. The more we see, the more we can gain from revelation given by God. I pray that you can use these for your learning and adaptation.

1. Prayer is putting oneself in submission to God to find out His Will concerning the matter at hand or the reason why the person sought Him out in the first place.

2. Prayer is a communicative method applied to know God's Mind.

3. Prayer is an act of submission to God.

4. Prayer is the surrendering of one's will, thoughts, and desires to receive God's.

5. Prayer is a pathway through which we can find God.

6. Prayer is a 2-sided mirror: one side allows us to see one's weaknesses, deficiencies, lack,

needs, etc. The other side to see God's Love, Strength, Ability, Attentiveness, Care, etc.

7. Prayer is a filling station to refuel after being emptied.

8. Prayer is a spiritual battlefield for conquering, and experiencing victories.

9. Prayer is a gateway of the supernatural, to send requests and receive results.

10. Prayer is building spiritual structures in and around our lives.

11. Prayer is the pen used to rewrite destiny according to God's Pattern.

12. Prayer is a spiritual investment with guaranteed rewards and returns.

13. Prayer is an arsenal for warfare against all enemies.

14. Prayer is the linguistic tool of the heart, keeping it plain and simple in all honesty with God.

15. Prayer is the incubator for spiritual pregnancy of God's desires to be birthed out through us.

16. Prayer is a protective wall against infiltrations and fiery darts of the wicked one.

17. Prayer is the Declaration of God's Word from our lips to create His Purpose.

There is so much more about prayer that you can add to this list to develop your prayer lifestyle. I suggest you search for Scriptures for these points to strengthen your knowledge of them as well. You will not need to memorize them, just meditate on them as God leads you. Once you understand the imagery, they will be applied naturally as you pray.

Concerning Hannah, I'm sure by now you, like myself, can call her meeting 'a prayer meeting'. It was not like the ones most are accustomed to; when we invite others to pray or are invited to pray. Hannah's meeting was not a general assembly call to prayer. It was a meeting with God and, it was private. Hannah met God in more ways than expected through her prayer meeting. How?

For starters, there was a releasing of what had been weighing heavy on her for years. During the meeting, she was not stuck nor lost for words. Everything flowed out of her, and the results were divine answers, and changes for destinies and generations.

It was the doing of the Lord. He allowed Hannah to reach to her end, and the end of herself. He waited for her to go past her situation, enemies, family, priests and self. God waited for Hannah; not the Hannah who had been burdened all those years, but the Hannah who was being birthed out from a place of pain and bitterness.

A new Hannah was arising. A destiny change creator was coming forth from eternity into time. Thus, by the time of this particular meeting, she was ready to spill it all out and didn't care what she looked like or who thought what about her. She was before God, and God was there. That was all that mattered.

Hannah knew it. The sense of being in God's Presence enabled her to express herself freely and honestly. This is what she said according to 1 Samuel 1: 11, *"O Lord of hosts, if thou wilt indeed look on the affliction of thine handmaid, and remember me, and not forget thine handmaid, but wilt give unto thine handmaid a man child, then I will give him unto the Lord all the days of his life, and there shall no razor come upon his head."* She addressed God, and worshipped Him as One Who is capable of doing great things. Did she see God standing or sitting there physically? I strongly doubt it. But she knew He was there, and had been there before she uttered those words that the Bible recorded.

Definitely, those were not the only words that Hannah pronounced out of her mouth although they were the only ones recorded during that time of prayer. The verse above states that Hannah prayed onto the Lord and wept sore. It was after releasing the agony of her soul that she made the solemn vow to the Lord.

There is no recollection of God responding to Hannah with audibility or by some great visible sign, yet, He did respond. How? Very simply by working through her after He had worked in her. We do not see the dealings of God within our spirit being, but He is there working.

He works by giving us His attention and strength to endure, while lending His helping hand to release the burden. Likewise, the Spirit of God moved in the being of Hannah. But the fine details of exactly how He did it, I do not know and will not attempt to do so. Certain things are kept secret by God until His timing of revealing. For now, I know He worked internally for external manifestations.

I say this because, the supernatural dealings of God are often unexplainable through words. Even the one who is going through the experience will find it difficult to express what is really taking place within. But much revelation can be pulled from Hannah's actions of crying and lip movements. Perhaps, her body posture while in prayer could deliver more insight on the cords that were being broken off her life by the Hand of the Lord. But unfortunately, the Bible does not describe that either.

I can only state through the eyes of the Spirit, by what He permits me to see, that there was a transformational process taking place during this meeting of prayer to God. There was no way Hannah could have made such a vow if God had not moved her to. Hannah transitioned from bitterness and affliction to taking responsibility of the things that pertain to God. She went from self, and concentration of her own needs, to a place of sacrificial offering unto the Lord. She not only released the cares of her soul and what could satisfy her, she released the very answer to the prayers she had been praying all along. Hannah saw God and God touched her. This is what I call a powerful prayer meeting.

No longer were her eyes glued on herself. It was no longer about how to prove anything to anyone nor how to gain favor with her husband. It was all about pleasing God with her life. Hannah offered herself through the very thing she would treasure most above all others, a child.

What happened to move Hannah so strongly? Well, there was an influence that spoke louder than any other voice Hannah had ever heard. This influence was stronger than the taunts of Peninnah, the stagnation of her situation, the love of her husband, and even the lust of the flesh. It left her broken and expressively helpless. She was where God needed her to be, a living sacrifice upon the altar of worship. Beautiful!

This altar was the only place for the great exchange to transpire. It was the ideal location for her to gain entrance into the Plan of God. There was no other way and no other ability. She had to be sacrificed along with whatever else she had. But in Truth, Hannah had nothing; not even herself. The FATHER had taken control.

Through wisdom imparted to her by God, she spoke. See this dear friend, God will not leave us forsaken, especially when we are in such a state of helplessness. To us, it may appear as if all is lost and there is no one to help. Some might eventually grow hopeless. But to God, this condition is where the believer, who is the seeker in prayer, can see His Light and Love like never before. David said in Psalm 51:16-17, *"For thou desirest not sacrifice; else would I give it: thou delightest not in burnt offering. The sacrifices of God are a broken spirit: a broken and a contrite heart, O God, thou wilt not despise."* A broken and contrite heart. That's the right condition of sacrificial lives.

Hannah was in this condition, and received more than what she could have ever imagined. Hannah received a new heart, a lightweight soul, and a sacrificial offering. But there was a mystery to the sacrificial offering she offered to God apart from herself. The mystery unfolded in that place of sacrifice. And with God's help I will shine light on its revealing.

You cannot give what you do not have. However, there is an exception to this rule, and that is if you're giving it by faith. Which means, releasing something from the future that is potentially yours, in the now. *"Now, faith is the substance of things hoped for and the evidence of things not seen"* according to Hebrews 11:1. The present is now, and if what can be given is not physically present, faith can work as the substitute until it comes. Faith stands as the collateral for the future, and for future appearances of things hoped for and prayed for; including vows of promises like what Hannah offered.

It was faith that Hannah offered as a vow. She did not have a son, not even a pregnancy, but she vowed a son as an offering while she laid on that altar of sacrifice. Hannah's transformation was faith-based. This is the result of prayer, obtaining the future ***now*** that will change destinies.

Listen, when all hope is gone, take from God what He can gave. Grasp hold of Who and What He is, *Faith-Seed*. He is the *Now-Substance* of our future hope. He releases Himself into our spirit, and leads us to declare with our mouths the new things we can believe for, which is patterned to His Will. But it can only occur when we die to ourselves, and everything else that has stood in the way.

Hannah went to a prayer meeting. It was there that she took from God what only He could give, and she received it by faith; because it was faith. If I can put it in another way, she borrowed from God a son and vowed how she would repay Him. The substance of faith she borrowed was in a form of a son. She actually formed the substance according to the pattern God gave her. It was formless until she as a borrower was able to form it.

Faith substance is Spirit-substance. It can become, or be created into whatever God wants it to be. Through prayer, it takes shape in and to the person in need. Once that seeker obtains it, he or she then releases it into the atmosphere permitting it to manifest within the earth realm.

Hannah's prayer meeting was truly rewarding. What if Hannah did not show up? What would have happened if she had refused to pray again? Imagine if the obstacles she went through had prevailed in keeping her from her pursuit. Hannah would have never made it to the destiny God had for her. That day, she became a partner in God's business.

The meeting was not only successful for Hannah, it was also pleasing to God. His Plan would have been fulfilled regardless of Hannah making it to the meeting or not, because God will not change His Plan even though He may change the vessels. I believe that it was pleasing to the Lord because Hannah was not an alternative, but rather, a selection by grace. And having His vessels of choice fulfill their individual destiny is well pleasing to the Father.

Aren't you glad that Father Himself attends to our business? Whether in the person of Yeshua, or Holy Spirit, He handles it. The Bible says that He is always attentive to our prayers, and I know that He answers at times even before we ask. He is our Loving Father.

With bewilderment, I find it difficult to ignore the fact that Eli was present in the Temple, but he was not in the meeting. He watched Hannah pray, and of course, inquired as to how long she will be drunk. But that was not God's question to her. Chapter 1 verse 12 states that Hannah continued praying before the Lord while Eli was watching her. He became a spectator, instead of a participator in what God was doing to transform destinies. This confirms my belief that there are things that only God can do, and man will have to be left out of the picture.

Seemingly, Eli interrupted Hannah's prayer, but he could not hinder her destiny. The Lord Himself was in the Temple and Hannah had direct access to Him. The meeting in itself along with the enormity of what was happening could not be interrupted. Therefore, everyone present, participants and spectators, had to come into alignment with the Will of God, including Eli. Therefore at the end, Eli spoke in verse 17 and said, *"Go in peace: and the God of Israel grant thee thy petition that thou hast asked of Him."* Thank God he was there to give the benediction, and that too was the Lord's doing.

What a relief for Hannah. The Bible states that after speaking with Eli, she left and went to eat. Her countenance began to show that she had been with the Lord for she was relieved of all sadness. What a way to end a meeting. Hannah attended the meeting one way, and she left a completely different person.

I pray that this will be the state of every believer who goes before the Lord in expectation of receiving something from Him. It is my prayer that should you ever be burdened with cares, or the desire for things that are rightfully yours, you will receive God's appointed portion for your life. It is our Father's desire to grant us all of His Kingdom. Therefore, as

Apostle Paul enlightened us, no good thing will God withhold from those who are in Christ Jesus and are called according to His Purpose in Love. These are the words of God and may they be marvelous in your eyes.

The Answers

8

Fruitful is what Hannah became after the meeting she had with God. No longer would she be labeled as Hannah the barren wife of Elkanah. Never again to be tormented by anyone including Peninnah. Everything was working cohesively together to accommodate Hannah's good and promising destiny.

Faithfully, Hannah did not receive only an answer, she received answers. God gave Hannah answers for herself, her son, and for Israel. She received a child, but included with the child was a prophetic destiny change in Hannah's life. By this I mean, Hannah began to operate in the prophetic. Interestingly, this prophetic nature had always been in Hannah, but it was locked.

Buried deep in her womb was a prophet, a priest, and a king. Everything was there awaiting a set time to be birthed out. Hannah carried more in her than all the children of Peninnah, more than the 10 sons Elkanah wished he was to her, and more than the child she desired. Hannah carried Israel's destiny, and she was made a mother in Israel.

Never overlook yourself because of problems, weaknesses, or the circumstances in which you find yourself. If you do, you may overlook what God can do through you. As long as you can get your eyes off yourself and turn them towards God, you will see what only He can do because of what He has done.

Hannah's answers were right there with her, but she could not see them because of everything else that clouded her vision. She had God all along; but instead of joy, she experienced bitterness and sadness. As a generational benefactor, I am grateful for the meeting with God that transformed Hannah's life.

Answers to prayers take various shapes and forms. The substance of faith is pliable and can transform into results God desires. Our part is to believe that He can do it. *"But without faith it is impossible to please Him: for he that cometh to God must believe that He is, and that He is a rewarder of them that diligently seek Him."* Hebrews 11:6.

Hannah was not yet pregnant physically, but by faith, she began to experience a change in her countenance. She became alive again. Her trip back home was quite different from how she had traveled to the Temple. She came burdened, but was returning fulfilled. Do you realize that Hannah had her answers long before she became intimate with her husband again? Most definitely. The answers were in her soul and heart. Faith now reigned.

Do you know that there are times people have faith but cannot see the answers because other properties are present? True faith will create the necessary works required. However, if there are other spirits like doubt and fear in a person, what then are mixed in with the works of faith? That person is double-minded, and cannot receive anything from the Lord as the apostle James said.

This is why God has to process us to establish purity in our thoughts and actions. It will result in praying righteous prayers. One cannot claim to operate in faith, and yet have doubts as to whether God will answer or not. An individual that prays, but does not believe that God loves him or her, will find it difficult to accept that God cares enough to fulfill his or her heart's desire no matter how innocent those desires are. Certain criterions have to be met.

Receiving the answers is just as important as requesting them. Both postures have to be equal in faith. I don't think that one should bother asking if he or she does not believe that the answers will be forthcoming. Unless maybe, the request was not according to God's Will in the first instance; and that's another story all together.

I do however suggest that when we are not sure of God's Perfect Will as it pertains to our prayer requests, we should still make them known to God trusting that Holy Spirit will reconstruct them appropriately. He is able to guide us even as we pray, and pray for us when we cannot do so. Moreover, He gives us faith or activates faith within us when we lack.

Anything God gives us is always more than we can request. He lavishes us with good things and does so exceedingly and abundantly. God is a Father Who takes pleasure in satisfying us with good things. Ask, and keep asking according to His Plan; but do so in faith. And when you're done asking, receive your answers in faith.

Look at Hannah. It was faith of receiving that allowed her to return home fulfilled. She believed that God had taken over Eli's tongue and spoke through him. For how can a man change from misinterpreting her actions of prayer and then pronounce a blessing upon her? It could have only been God on Hannah's side, ensuring that there was no interruption to His Will being done. Again, all things and all persons had to conform to His Divine Agenda.

The barrenness was broken and she was pregnant with and by faith. You see, Hannah was not only barren physically, she was also barren spiritually. So, although Hannah was not physically pregnant, she was spiritually pregnant with the Word from the Lord; a Word of Faith. This was the first thing which had to happen and God performed it.

She worshipped along with her family early the next morning before returning home. I'm of the opinion that even her worship was different, being more true than ever before. It was filled with faith that produced gratitude to God in advance for what He had already done.

With this connection of faith, Hannah returned home. It produced the Lord's remembrance of her during the moment of intimacy between she and her husband. God was mindful of Hannah and granted

Hannah her heart's desire which was a son who was named, Samuel.

The child was graced by God with anointings and mantles that were uncommon. Samuel was the last official judge of Israel, and one of its most powerful prophets. The Bible indicates that not one word of Samuel fell to the ground. Which means God honored every word that Samuel spoke. However, Samuel was not to be born from the bitterness still present in his mother. He could only have been born from the new Hannah.

After his birth, the new Hannah was able to remain faithful to the vow she made to the Lord. She took responsibility for the things pertaining to the Lord's house. The Bible says that Hannah began to go every year to take a garment to Samuel. In other words, she became committed to what she had committed to the Lord. And that place of commitment was also her worship unto God.

Hannah transformed into a minister by ministering to the priest, Samuel. Yes, he was her son physically, but spiritually he was her authority and spiritual covering appointed by God. Ministration unto him was a form of stewardship unto the Lord. But Hannah had to keep pure before she could approach the future priest, and even provide garments for him. This was because God ordained everything about the priesthood as holy, even to their garments. Thus, the transformation she received during her meeting with the Lord produced answers in multiple ways. And one of them was the change of destiny she entered into by becoming a minister to the Lord through her service to His priest and prophet, Samuel.

Later in Chapter 2, the Lord shows us Hannah's appearance as a prophetess. Hannah prays, but this time her prayer is different. Hannah prays according to the new Hannah that God has destined her to be. Her proximity to God is changed based on the new posture of her heart. Instead of a heart of bitterness, which results in being far from God, Hannah's heart is given to insights into the things of God. She is now one who stands before the Lord. That is, her spirit was able to know more of the Plan of God as it pertained to her generation and the ones to follow.

1 Samuel 2:1 reads, *"And Hannah prayed, and said, my heart rejoiceth in the Lord, my horn is exalted in the Lord: my mouth is enlarged over my enemies; because I rejoice in my salvation."* What a testimony it is to go from a person bitter in soul to a person rejoicing in heart. It's no longer her soul speaking. Now she is speaking from her heart. And she's rejoicing in the Lord. No longer is she focused on herself. Now she has God as her focus.

Friend, was it not Hannah just a few years or a few months ago whose words could not come out so audible? Her mouth was too heavy to open whilst praying, but now her mouth is enlarged. Hannah is now what I can call *a woman on fire*. The real prayer warrior arose, and she moved mightily in the realm of the prophetic. She said in 1 Samuel 2:3-5,

> *Talk no more so exceeding proudly; let not arrogancy come out of your mouth: for the LORD is a God of knowledge, and by Him actions are weighed. The bows of the mighty men are broken, and they that stumbled are girded with strength. They that were full have hired out themselves for bread; and they that were hungry ceased: so that the barren hath born seven; and she that hath many children is waxed feeble.*

When you look at the number seven, it is the number of completion and perfection. Hannah was complete and made perfect when she faced God. It produced God's Mind and Plan for Israel.

Astonishingly, Hannah's prophetic voice projected louder towards the end of her prayer, and with tremendous Revelation. God had apprehended her into the Realm of Prophetic Intercession. That is, the ability to receive prayer points from God to pray them on earth. We can also see her operating in Prophetic Warfare; another prayer strategy. 1 Samuel

2:10 records her praying as such, *"The adversaries of the Lord shall be broken to pieces; out of heaven shall He thunder upon them: the LORD shall judge the ends of the earth; and He shall give strength on to His king, and exalt the horn of His anointed."*

Question please. Who is the *king* and *anointed one* that Hannah is referring to? I'm asking because Israel had no king when Hannah prayed this prayer. So, what was she doing? That's right. Hannah was operating prophetically as God gave her utterance. I would like to think that there were aspects of the apostolic engaged too.

Hannah had moved into the Mind of God concerning the future of Israel with groundbreaking pronouncements of its Kingship Dimension. I told you earlier that Hannah carried kingship in her womb; her spiritual womb that is. And thus, we read about her activating that Kingship Anointing over Israel before it even happened in the earth realm. She was a doorway for God to pass through to present Himself as the King of Israel. And when she prayed, all realms *(spiritual and physical, good and evil)* heard what Hannah declared by God.

No wonder the enemy hurried in with an attempt to pollute and destroy the Plan of God's Kingship Realm being established in Israel. In doing so, satan blindly moved the people to request a king right before God could give them His king. *"And the LORD said unto Samuel, Hearken unto the voice of the people in all that they say unto thee: for they have not rejected thee, but they have rejected me, that I should not reign over them" (1 Samuel 8:7).* This was evil at work. Their rebellion to God and rejection of Him for Saul's kingship, surfaced all the more when Saul rebelled as well. Fortunately, for Israel, God later chose David, a man after God's heart.

David was God's king, and anointed one that Hannah prophesied. It was his horn that was exalted by God. Hannah was on key with this prophetic word, and it happened because she was on key with God. An ordinary housewife was what she was, but a prophetic voice was who she became through the power of prayer.

Additionally, the transformation of Hannah's life was so peculiar that she moved from a place of remembrance by God to a place of visitations from Him. Someone who was forgotten, was now being visited by the Holy One of Israel to bring about a fullness to Hannah's life and happiness. What she borrowed from the Lord, she paid in full. And what God received from her, He gave back abundantly. God was Faithful, and gave Hannah more than she could have ever given to Him.

The Bible informs us that Hannah was visited by God in the area of childbearing; not once, but multiple times. She gave birth to three sons and two daughters in addition to Samuel. She had given God one and He blessed her with five more. Hannah moved from Mercy to Grace.

Hannah's destiny change transcended realms. It was partly due to what God did through her life that the Glory of God was restored to Israel in later years. Eli's sons had been the cause of the Ark of the Covenant being lost to Israel; signifying the departure of the Glory. However, that was just the aftermath, because the Glory had lifted long before the battle between Israel and Philistine. There was a void since the time of Samuel's childhood in the Temple; because the Bible states in 1 Samuel 3 that the Word of the Lord was scarce, and there was no open vision. God's Presence had departed. No Word equates to no vision, because, there was no Presence.

Samuel's service to God of purity and holiness brought back the Glory to Israel. It is appropriate to say that because of Samuel, the Glory returned. God was able to find one person who was righteous before Him. And God will always look for one; just as He looked for the one called Hannah who was desperately crying out to Him for a child. And she trusted that God would do it for her.

When we pray, we pray for answers and we trust that we will get the answers we've prayed for; because we trust that God can do it. But as I pen these words, I have come to see that when we pray, we are actually praying for destiny changes, and not just simply answers. The answers we suppose we are expecting are really coming as answers to transform our lives. Thus, prayer can no longer be considered as what folks thought it was. There is absolutely more to it.

It was through studying the life of Hannah that the Holy Spirit opened my eyes to see the real power of prayer. I can no longer believe that a great prayer warrior is one who simply gets answers to prayers. No, that is not a great prayer warrior.

A great prayer warrior is one who allows the answers he or she has prayed for to transform his or her life. A person is not a great prayer warrior, or great in any regard, if he or she has not been greatly changed by God every time there was a personal prayer meeting.

So, I urge you my beloved, do not approach prayer again as a means to get an answer for something you desire. Come to prayer with the yielded heart for what God can do in transforming you into His Will and Divine Purpose. Never conclusively set your mind or heart on what you think your answers should be. Always keep yourself opened to the answers that God wants to give. When you comply to this format, you will never leave the meeting without at least one answer.

Leave your meeting with God with a vision of what God wants you to see in accordance to His Will and Purpose. He will use our desires to get our attention. And when He has our attention, He will deliver to us a *Now* Word of Faith to impregnate us. Once you lay hold of it, be very fast in releasing it back to Him just like Hannah did. Don't hold on to it, because, if you do you might not get more of what He has to offer.

I will end this Chapter with a clear word of encouragement. God allowed you to read this book, *Hannah PRAYED: And Changed Destiny,* because there is a destiny change waiting for you and awaiting you. I declare over your life a divine change in your destiny. May God saturate you with things pertaining to His Israel. May He elevate you to gain access into His Kingship Anointing in all pureness and majesty.

Remain mindful, when you begin to experience this Apostolic and Prophetic Declaration, to give back to God all that He has bestowed upon you. If you do not do that, the vision will become more than you can bear. Hannah's example is to also show that we have to give birth to whatever God gives us. The essence of you receiving what He gives is that you release it back to Him. Only He can bring it to fruition and cause it to mature. If you keep it, you won't birth it.

Do not fear that you are losing something that God has given to you. No, you are not. By given it up, you are only getting it back in multiplicity and abundance. This act is your way of showing God that you trust Him.

Be like Abraham was when it came to Isaac, his son. Abraham was willing to sacrifice him just as God had commanded. He knew that God gave Isaac to him, but he also was wise enough to know that Isaac never belonged to him. He and Isaac both belonged to God. Thus, Abraham's obedience with Isaac was a type and shadow of Yeshua, God's sacrificed Lamb.

There is a song that the Holy Ghost gave me some years ago. It's titled, *I Lay Me Down,* because that was exactly what I needed to do; lay myself down along with the vision God had given me. But before then, I had been carrying it as if it was my responsibility to fulfill. Thus, I began to perceive it with worries and doubts as if it could not happen.

I was fourteen years old when God gave the vision, or at least, when I saw that there was more to my life. For years later, I struggled in labor pains. I didn't realize that by doubting myself, I was indirectly doubting God's ability, and questioning His choice of vessel to use, me. It was not until I was thirty that I received a visitation from God, to teach me that all I needed to do was to lay it down at His Feet.

In that meeting, He said that He had to train me to give the vision back to Him, because it is *His* vision. That's why it appeared big in magnitude of fulfillment, and overwhelming to me. I cannot do anything for God if He does not do it through me. As a result of the lesson, I wrote and recorded the song. Today, it serves as a reminder to me that God is All in All, Beginning and End. He is also the Center. I must keep myself laid down before Him.

You see, God will give you something that is far bigger than you, because He wants you to realize that you cannot handle it, and neither can you bring it to past. He wants you to know that it originated in Him, and you must depend on Him to fulfill it in and through you.

So, every vision that God has given you, every word, and everything that you have sensed in your heart that has not come to full completion, give them back to God. Dedicate them to Him, cast them down at His Feet in total surrender. Remember, you have to conform to the answers He wants to give you, and it is through prayers that you will see yourself transformed into His Will.

Hannah PRAYED, and Changed Destiny. Are you ready to be like Hannah? I hope you are. And, may the Lord bless you as you continue your spiritual journey in Him.

Personal Notes

The 'Servant' Author

Olivia Precious Cooper is the President of I Am Precious International (IAP) Harvest Ministries. She's called as an Apostle and Prophet of God. She provides mentoring to current and potential leaders. She is also a philanthropist, author, entrepreneur and psalmist. Apostle Precious ministers to bring God's Word forth with Anointing for understanding and daily application. Christ uses her to awaken His body by unlocking destinies, imparting mantles, delivering, and developing those called into ministry within His Kingdom. She presents her life as a conduit through which Holy Spirit creates spiritual transformation in attitudes and atmospheres by prophetic prayers, worship and utterances. Although, she is totally committed to the work of ministry, her greatest passion is to know God as she is known by Him.

For more information:
      https://www.preciousinternational.org/precious/
         precious@preciousinternational.org
Facebook: @OliviaPreciousCooper
Twitter: @PreciousIntl
Youtube: I Am Precious Intl. Harvest Ministries

Resources

We would like to recommend Audio Messages to accommodate Hannah PRAYED.

Hannah Prayed (Parts 1&2)
Killing the Root of Bitterness

I AM Precious International Harvest Ministries
- Sunday Glory Service
   For phone access to services:
   Dial +1(218)632-0947 pin 2010#

IAP Publishing is a branch of I Am Precious International Ministries creating Godly changes in attitudes and atmospheres.

More Books by Olivia Precious Cooper

The Invisible Image: *God's Makeover of the Heart* is a plea and challenge for men and women to come to God and discover their true nature in Him alone. Get answers to the three most important questions: Who am I? Where did I come from? Where am I going? This tool is powerful, humorous, and practical.

IAP Publishing
ISBN-13: **978-0-9830157-9-6**

Kissed And Killed: *You too can rise from the grave of betrayal* is a must read as the Kiss of Betrayal is experienced in everyone's life. But how do you handle your trust being broken by a loved one? The Kiss did hurt but get empowered to live again, by gaining insight for your next great step.

IAP Publishing
ISBN-13: **978-0983015734**

Precious Living Words *(Parts 1 & 2)*

Precious Living Words I & II are both pages of revelations and understandings of the Scriptures that the Holy Spirit gave to Precious during some intimate moments. His Words have been a source of strength and she has decided to share these with you. The Spirit of God is in each word and you will receive life as you read and mediate on them.

IAP Publishing
ISBN-13: **978-0983015765**
ISBN-13: **978-0983015789**

Strength of The Woman: *Her Making*

This is the first volume in this series. Strength of The Woman: *Her Making* is a Powerful Revelation to recreate your life. This first volume introduces you to the Making of The Woman. You will learn of The Woman, Adam's Woman, Eve, and God's Woman; your making determines your Strength.

IAP Publishing
ISBN-13: **978-0983015758**

You may also be interested in our Strength of The Woman Conference. For more information, visit
https://www.preciousinternational.org/events/womens-conference/

Order your copies today, as well as audio and video messages.

Services for Spiritual Growth

We have Powerful and Life changing events like Eagle Power Weekends, SOTW Women Conference and IAP Wealth Empowerment Seminars. Contact us to inquiries about them.

Website: **https://www.preciousinternational.org**

Phone: +1(615) 669-6460

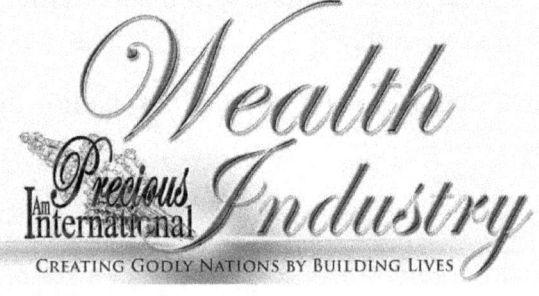

www.ingramcontent.com/pod-product-compliance
Lightning Source LLC
LaVergne TN
LVHW041626070426
835507LV00008B/464